Foreign Business Law in China

Past Progress and Future Challenges

Foreign Business Law in China
Past Progress and Future Challenges

Pitman B. Potter

University of British Columbia Law Faculty

Research sponsored by
The 1990 Institute

The
1990
Institute

The 1990 Institute
651 Gateway Boulevard, Suite 880
South San Francisco, CA 94080

Printed in the United States of America

Library of Congress Card Number: 94–74928

ISBN: 0–472–10637–6

Again, for Vicki

Contents

Foreword

The 1990 Institute is proud to present this book by Professor Pitman Potter. This is the first volume to be published as a result of The Institute's Phase II research on economic reform in China.

An important contribution of this book is its discussion not only of China's foreign trade and foreign investment laws, but also of the gaps between these laws and their actual performance. A scholar steeped in China's social and cultural values, Professor Potter approaches these gaps with an intimate understanding of the difficulties that face China in adjusting to the demands of the modern world and of the significant progress that has been made in the short span of fifteen years since reform began in 1979.

The book vividly illustrates the dynamics of this adjustment process in five subject areas: foreign trade, foreign investment, technology transfer and intellectual property rights, finance (foreign exchange and taxation), and dispute settlement—areas of great interest to the foreign business community and to the Chinese authorities as well. In view of the critical role that foreign trade and foreign investment have played in China's economic reform, how the tension in this continuing process of adjustment is resolved will surely have a significant impact on the future of the Chinese economy as well as on the fortunes of foreign business firms that trade with or invest in China.

The Institute's Phase I research was directed by Professor Walter Galenson of Cornell University; It focused on a comprehensive review of China's economic reform experience from 1978 to 1991. The results were published by The Institute in 1993 in *China's Economic Reform*, edited by Walter Galenson (ISBN 0–472–10473–X). The Phase II research, now underway, concentrates on six areas identfied by The Institute as of critical importance to further reform of the Chinese economy. In addition to the subject of this book, the other areas are: agriculture, enterprise, finance, labor, and taxation. The results of these research projects will be published by The Institute, as they are completed.

The Institute itself is a remarkable phenomenon. It was founded in 1990—hence its name—by a group of individuals in the United States that was deeply interested in China and wanted to help the people there without becoming involved in the politics of either country. They shared the conviction that the most effective way to improve the welfare of the people in China was through enhanced understanding of the social and economic barriers that have held back China's modernization. Though busy people themselves in their own professions, they freely contributed their time, talents, and money to establish this organization and tell others about it. Soon, support poured in from a wide variety of sources—individuals, small and medium-sized businesses, corporations, and large foundations—all through the efforts of volunteers who helped spread the word about The Institute in their precious spare time. The support has enabled The Institute to complete its Phase I research and to begin its Phase II research. Perhaps, nowhere else in the world is there a research institution dedicated to public policy research that is so completely based on grassroots support. It is a shining example of American volunteerism at work.

The founders and supporters of The Institute recognized from the beginning that all the idealism and good intentions would be of no avail if China's government were to ignore The Institute's research results. It took two years' patient and persistent effort to convince the authorities in China that The Institute was acting in China's best interest. Once acceptance was achieved, the door was thrown wide open.

In December 1992, The Institute presented the results of its Phase I research at conferences in Shanghai and Beijing. Among the participants at both conferences were senior government officials and eminent scholars who were advisors to policy makers. In April 1994, The Institute joined forces with the People's Bank of China, the nation's central bank, to organize and sponsor An International Conference on Bank Supervision and Commercial Bank Operations, in order to contribute to China's newly launched financial reform.

Similarly, the publication of this book is timed to serve as background material for An International Conference on China's Foreign Trade and Foreign Investment Laws to be held in San Francisco on March 24–25, 1995. The results of this conference will be presented at a subsequent conference to be held in Beijing one month later. The Beijing conference will be co-sponsored by the prestigious Western Returned Scholars Association in Beijing and the Ministry of Foreign Trade and Economic Cooperation, the government agency that is responsible for drafting laws and regulations on foreign trade and foreign investment in China and for supervising these activities. The publication of this book and the conferences that follow together constitute a concrete example of what The Institute seeks to do: service for the benefit of the 1.2 billion people of China and ultimately the people of the world.

The 1990 Institute invites other similarly-minded individuals and organizations to join its volunteer Associates in a common pursuit of this goal.

* * *

The 1990 Institute would like to thank Vision 2047 Foundation for their generous support of the printing and publication of this book and of the Chinese translation to be published in China. Vision 2047 Foundation, established in 1989, is a nonprofit, nonpartisan organization dedicated to promoting the long-term stability and prosperity of Hong Kong. The Foundation's effort is directed toward improving understanding of Hong Kong among decision makers worldwide in the transition to 1997 and beyond. We are most encouraged that the members of the Foundation and The Institute share a similar vision and goal.

Hang-Sheng Cheng
President, The 1990 Institute

San Francisco
December, 1994

Acknowledgments

This book began as a policy paper prepared at the request of The 1990 Institute. I would like to thank The Institute, and particularly C. B. Sung and Hang-Sheng Cheng, for their unflagging encouragement and support. Several law students at the University of British Columbia Law Faculty provided research assistance in connection with this project, including Jennifer Miller, Qi Xiaodong, Yan Yibing, and Yin Li. Mark Kremzner, a graduate student at the University of British Columbia, provided especially helpful research and writing assistance in preparing the first draft. Many friends and colleagues in China gave generously of their time to meet and discuss with me many of the issues addressed in this volume. I would also like to thank the members of The 1990 Institute's Review Committee and an anonymous reviewer, whose valuable comments helped me to improve the text. I am grateful as well to Rhona Johnson and Helen Wheeler for their careful and patient work in bringing the book to press. Finally, I would like to thank Vicki, without whose love and support this work would not have been possible. In spite of the assistance that I received on this project, errors no doubt remain for which I alone am responsible.

Pitman B. Potter

Vancouver
November 1994

Abbreviations

ALL	Administrative Litigation Law
ASEAN	Association of Southeast Asian Nations
BIT	bilateral investment treaty
CCPIT	China Council for the Promotion of International Trade
CIETAC	China International Economic and Trade Arbitration Commission
CITIC	China International Trust and Investment Corporation
CJVs	cooperative joint ventures
CPL	Civil Procedure Law of the People's Republic of China
BOC	Bank of China
ECL	Economic Contract Law
ETDZs	Economic and Technological Development Zones
EJVs	equity joint ventures
FEACs	Foreign Exchange Adjustment Centers
FEC	foreign exchange certificate
FECL	Foreign Economic Contract Law
FESCO	Foreign Enterprise Service Corporation
FETAC	Foreign Economic and Trade Arbitration Commission
FIEs	foreign investment enterprises
GPCL	General Principles of Civil Law

ICCT   Industrial and Commercial Consolidated Tax

IITL   Individual Income Tax Law of the People's Republic of China

IPR   intellectual property rights

JV   joint venture

JVITL   Joint Venture Income Tax Law

LDCs   less-developed countries

MOU   Memorandum of Understanding

MOFERT   Ministry of Foreign Economic Relations and Trade

MOFTEC   Ministry of Foreign Trade and Economic Cooperation

NFTCs   national foreign trade corporations

NPC   National People's Congress (NPC)

NRDVs   natural resource development ventures

PBOC   People's Bank of China

RMB   *renminbi*

SAE   State Administration of Exchange and Control

SAIC   State Administration for Industry and Commerce

SEZs   Special Economic Zones

UFETL   Unified Foreign Enterprise Tax Law

USTR   United States Trade Representative

VAT   value-added tax

WFOE   wholly foreign-owned enterprise

WIPO   World Intellectual Property Organization

CHAPTER 1

Introduction

I. The Law and Development Paradigm and Its Critics

The role of law in inducing economic growth has long been the focus of scholarly and policy activity. Based largely on Max Weber's correlation between the emergence of legal rationality and economic growth in Europe,[1] the field of law and development emerged in the 1960s with the aim of promoting economic growth and political stability in the developing world through the establishment of Western-style legal systems.[2] Scholars in this field suggested that the use of formal rules and institutions such as property and contract law would permit economic activity to be more predictable. Such predictability would, it was hoped, lead to entrepreneurship and risk taking, which in turn would permit capital accumulation and ultimately long-term economic growth.

Unfortunately many of the approaches suggested by the law and development scholars were not altogether successful.[3] This was due in part to factors external to the theory itself. These included the cold war, which gave primacy to political stability and loyalty to the United States over economic growth, essentially derailing efforts to build functioning legal systems in the developing world.[4] The oil embargo of the 1970s undermined the economic growth policies of many oil-dependent countries, and the subsequent collapse of world commodity prices placed additional strains on the developing economies that were still largely dependent on commodity exports.[5] A pattern of Third-World debt, caused largely by the difficult economic conditions in the developing world combined with the political interests of the United States and the economic interests of its commercial banks, exacerbated the obstacles to economic growth as debt service payments increasingly swallowed up the foreign exchange reserves that were slowly being accumulated.[6]

But there were also internal problems with the assumptions about the relationship between law and economic growth. First, the culture and history of many developing countries were not conducive to the ready acceptance of foreign legal systems. Although the elites who benefited from pre-World War II colonialism may have been prepared to accept foreign legal institutions, they sometimes indulged in nationalistic critiques of these institutions, both to preserve their own political power and in response to popular distrust of the appearance of postcolonial subjugation to foreign influences.[7] Western legal systems were often seen as entrenching the disparities of wealth that characterized much of the developing world.[8] Finally and perhaps most important, the norms inherent in much of Western law, whether imposed during the colonial period or adopted later on, were often incompatible with social customs and practices that informed local economic activity.[9]

Critiques of the law and development movement have tended to center on the gap between Western legal norms and local attitudes. Local economic actors did not easily assimilate the basic ideas of individual autonomy that are fundamental to Western formal law, which itself emerged in response to socioeconomic and political conditions specific to the European experience.[10] These basic ideas also tended to elude local governments that adopted Western-style legal systems, as the utilitarian goals of these regimes denied the emphasis on autonomy that underpinned Western legal norms.

II. Law and Development in the People's Republic of China

In the People's Republic of China (hereafter "PRC" or "China"), the regime has made explicit the linkage between legal reform and economic reform.[11] Yet among Chinese communities generally, there exists a significant gap between foreign legal norms and local practices where informal ties based on notions of relationships (*guanxi*) and personal empathy (*ganqing*) have been a dominant factor in economic life.[12] Drawing on a historical tradition in which formal legal rules were not the source of norms governing contract and property relations, Chinese communities relied extensively on family networks and clan and guild rules to set the standards for commercial behavior.[13] This affected not only the structure of these relationships but also their consequences, as economic activities were seen as involving long-term relationships rather than short-term transactional consequences. The formation of agreements has tended to be based on informal promises, whereas enforcement has been achieved through flexible processes that take into account the circumstances of both parties.[14] Disputes are handled informally and typically involve compromise by both parties in order to preserve their long-term relationships. In the economy of scarcity that has characterized the PRC, these relational approaches have been essential, since access to raw materials, bureaucratic largesse, and markets has depended more on political rather than economic resources.

The reform policies in China since 1978 have created the foundation for change, as market forces have been permitted to play a greater role and a money economy has gradually replaced the planned quota economy of the Maoist period.[15] Complementing these economic reforms has been a vigorous effort at legal reform.[16] China's recent efforts at entry to the General Agreement on Tariffs and Trade (GATT) and the World Trade Organization (WTO) have given rise to additional reforms. Although it is evident that many people in China both welcome the legal reforms of the post-Mao period and have adjusted their activities to take them into account, it is also evident that old customs have been slow to fade, and relational economic activities are still dominant over transactional ties.[17] These obstacles to the success of domestic legal reform were not surprising, but they do impose on the current regime the challenge of adapting new policies and new rules to existing customs and practices.

In the context of China's foreign economic relations, the issue is more complex. As part of its economic reform policies, China has opened itself to the outside world and encouraged the expansion of commercial ties with the international economy. While debate continues over the substance of the reforms, many changes were in fact made.[18] Licensing and tariff requirements on imports were reduced and the state trading system was changed in order to reduce central government involvement (chiefly through indirect subsidies) in production and sales of Chinese-made goods in the international market.[19] The foreign exchange system was reformed in order to permit market forces to play a greater role in setting exchange rates.[20] Changes were made in the treatment of foreign investment enterprises and their access to the Chinese domestic market.[21] The Chinese legal system's approach to foreign trade and investment was continually revised and improved.[22] As well, domestic economic reforms have been aimed at reducing state subsidies and improving efficiency in part so as to strengthen China's ability to compete in the international marketplace.[23]

The Chinese government has used formal law and regulation to induce foreign business ties in several ways. By portraying itself as a regime that accepts the rule of law, the Chinese government has hoped to encourage foreign business interests to downplay the political risks of participating in China's economic growth. By allowing specific legal regimes to govern its foreign economic relations, China has hoped to establish clear and predictable frameworks for foreign business. By providing specific preferences in its laws, the government has hoped to induce foreign business activities in various targeted geographic areas and commercial sectors. Yet questions remain as to the effects that these legal reforms have had in the past and will have in the future on foreign business activity in China.

III. Scope of Analysis

With each of the issues just discussed as background, this book will address the more specific issue of the role of law in five areas of China's foreign economic relations: international trade, investment, technology transfer, taxation and foreign exchange, and dispute resolution. Although other topics no doubt could be included, the areas selected provide useful parameters for the discussion of the role of law in China's foreign economic relations. Based on these selections, each of the five substantive chapters in this volume addresses the content, performance, and underlying attitudes of the applicable legal regime. The content of the legal regime is an important reference point for analysis, as it sets forth the ideals that are supposed to govern. The content of the legal regime in each of the topic areas is analyzed by looking at the texts of applicable laws and regulations, as well as policy statements and other less formal rules.[24] Inquiry about performance tells us how these ideals are being carried out, while examination of attitudes provides insights as to the factors driving performance. The performance of the legal system may be analyzed through case studies and interviews,[25] and experience in the operation of the legal regimes in practice. Attitudes about the various legal regimes may be determined through examining policy discussions, behavior in economic relationships, and through interviews and other personal inquiries. With these data as background, an assessment will be made of the implications in each of the target areas for the role of law in China's foreign economic relations. The book will conclude with a series of policy proposals for increasing the performance of China's foreign economic law systems.

An analysis of this breadth necessarily entails a significant level of generalization, to which there will undoubtedly be specific exceptions. There has been marked regional variation in China's development experience, such that the record in major centers such as Beijing and Shanghai cannot be assumed to mirror that in all other regions. Similarly the trend toward decentralization of political power that has characterized the past few years adds additional complexity to the overall picture. However, an analysis of the Chinese foreign economic relations regime can still proceed usefully from a discussion of the general characteristics of national-level regulations. Not only are these the framework upon which local regulations are based, or at least the norms against which they react, but the prospects and problems identified with regard to national-level regulations also establish basic criteria by which local variations might be examined in a subsequent project. Thus, although reference will be made to the role of local officials in interpreting and implementing central regulations, this analysis will not attempt to offer an in-depth treatment of local regulations as variations on central management of foreign economic relations.

Finally, it is important to note that the reform process in China is ongoing. The time frame used for the purposes of this discussion concludes at the end of 1993, although occasional reference will be made to events in 1994. It is certain that many of the problems and reforms suggested herein are already under consideration within Chinese decision-making circles, and important changes (most notably the foreign exchange reforms effective January 1, 1994) have begun to be implemented. Nonetheless, it is hoped that in addition to reviewing the first fifteen years of reform in the role of law in China's foreign economic relations, this effort will provide a basis upon which to examine and assess future developments.

IV. Issues Generic to Law and Foreign Business in China

A number of issues cut across the boundaries between the issues discussed in this book. These include (1) basic approaches to the role of law in China, (2) laws of general application, (3) administrative reform, and (4) foreign influences, each of which has an effect on the regulation of China's foreign economic relations. A brief discussion of these issues will provide important context for the subsequent discussion.

A. Basic Approaches to the Role of Law

The Chinese legal regime for managing foreign economic relations is governed by basic approaches that emphasize instrumentalism and formalism in the content and operation of law. Law is conceived of as an instrument of rule, whereas the effectiveness of this instrument is subject to formalistic assessments that emphasize content over performance.

Instrumentalism in Chinese Law

The Chinese government's approach to law is fundamentally instrumentalist.[26] This means that laws and regulations are intended to be instruments of policy enforcement. Legislative and regulatory enactments are not intended as expressions of immutable general norms that apply consistently in a variety of human endeavors, and neither are they constrained by such norms. Rather, laws and regulations are enacted explicitly to achieve immediate policy objectives of the regime. Law is not a limit on state power; it is a mechanism by which state power is exercised.

This approach to the role of law derives from a long tradition in Chinese history, extending from the Confucianism of Imperial China to Republicanism of China under the Kuomintang and finally to the Marxism-Leninism of China after 1949, where law has been used primarily to achieve social control but also to pursue economic goals.[27] Throughout the 1950s in the PRC, law and regulation were used to transform the economy and society to achieve the revolutionary goals of the Maoist regime.[28] The regime's instrumentalism was amply illustrated when, just at the time law began to be taken seriously not simply as an instrument of rule but as a source of norms and principles of general applicability that might give rise to rights and protections for the populace, it was subjected to criticism for obstructing the policy goals of the party and state.[29]

In the post-Mao era, efforts at legal reform have been couched mainly in the language of instrumentalism—in part so as to enlist the support of conservative members of the regime who question the benefits of a legal system that intrudes on the Party's monopoly on power.[30] The resilience of the instrumentalist notion of rule by law, as opposed to a universalist approach to the rule of law is widely acknowledged today by the legal communities in China as a matter severely in need of reform.[31]

The basic philosophy of instrumentalism that informs the Chinese legal system applies in particular to foreign economic relations. The enactment of laws and regulations on trade, investment, technology transfer, and other matters was aimed at achieving specific policy results, without necessarily any reliance on or reference to broader legal principles. To find expressions of this instrumentalism, one need look no further than the laws themselves, where the centrality of the regime's policy goals is entrenched in the general principles of virtually every enactment.[32] Another example lies in the circumstances leading to the enactment of the General Principles of Civil Law (GPCL), where the National People's Congress (NPC) Standing Committee Chair Peng Zhen was told that Japanese investors would not commit capital to China unless there was a civil code in place, and then returned to China and directed the GPCL drafters to shelve their wrangling and complete the drafting of the law. The code was enacted shortly thereafter.

One consequence of legal instrumentalism as practiced in China is that laws and regulations are intentionally ambiguous so as to provide policymakers and implementing officials alike significant flexibility in interpretation and implementation.[33] Many of the laws and regulations governing China's foreign economic relations are replete with vague passages that do not lend predictability or transparency to the regulatory process.[34] In part, this works to free the hands of central policymakers to modify the policy foundations for these measures and permits local implementing officials to use broad discretion in ensuring that regulatory enforcement satisfies policy objectives. While regulatory ambiguities may benefit foreign business interests, they also make uniform interpretation and enforcement difficult if not impossible to obtain.

The Role of Formalism

The instrumentalist bent of current policies of legal reform is complemented by the role of formalism in the assessment of the effects of law. Formalism in this sense means that the content of law is assumed to represent reality, with little if any inquiry permitted into gaps between the content and operation of law.[35] Law is seen not only as a tool by which desired social, economic, and political goals can be attained, but also is presumed to be an *effective* tool. Where a policy is agreed upon and then expressed through law or regulation, the law or regulation serves as a conclusive indicator that the policy is being enforced.

Thus, in the area of foreign business relations, Chinese legal treatises seldom if ever address in depth or detail the gap between doctrine and practice.[36] China's description of its foreign trade and investment practices in response to inquiries from GATT members was based largely on a recitation of regulatory pronouncements whose effective enforcement was widely disputed by foreign businesses.[37] This approach was evident most recently in the White Paper on Intellectual Property, issued by the Chinese government in June 1994.[38]

To a large extent this formalism is a predictable consequence of the instrumentalism that drives the enactment of law and regulation. Although consensus is difficult enough to achieve concerning the legislative and regulatory enactments that are expressions of policy ideals, it is nearly impossible to achieve in the area of implementational details due to the numerous political trade-offs that accompany policy enforcement.[39] As a result, policies and the laws and regulations that express them are replete with thinly veiled compromises that represent programmatic ideals rather than implementational details. Where elaborate inquiry into implementation is likely to raise issues that may threaten the political consensus or even the policy ideals, such inquiry is not pursued. Rather, the content of law is seen as coterminous with its operational effects. In China's contentious policy environment, the ideal and its implementation become one.

B. Laws of General Application

China's foreign economic relations are subject to a broad array of laws of general application. The 1985 Foreign Economic Contract Law of the PRC (FECL), for example, applies to all foreign-related contracts, whether they involve foreign trade, foreign investment, or technology transfer.[40] The Economic Contract Law (ECL), enacted in 1981 and revised in 1993, governs purely domestic contracts, including those signed between foreign investment enterprises and other Chinese units.[41] Other laws and regulations of specific application play an important role in each of these types of transactions, as well as in the areas of finance and dispute resolution. But the contractual relations are set by the FECL, which embodies the general philosophy of instrumentalism discussed earlier. The effect of the FECL in turn is qualified by China's accession to the UN Convention on Contracts for the International Sales of Goods, which China joined effective January 1, 1988, and which contains many principles derived from European commercial law that augment and in some instances displace FECL provisions in instances where the foreign contracting party is from a state party to the Convention.[42]

As the distinction between the FECL and the ECL suggests, the Chinese legal regime makes a basic distinction between laws applicable domestically and laws applicable to foreign matters. However, this distinction is gradually breaking down. For example, the General Principles of Civil Law, enacted in 1986, contains provisions for contract and property relations involving both domestic and foreign economic relations.[43] This law is of particular importance to foreign transactions because of its choice of law rules which, in conjunction with the FECL, permit foreign parties broad freedom to select the governing law in trade transaction (although Chinese law must govern in foreign investment transactions). The law also contains important doctrinal rules on legal capacity, contract and property relations, and the consequences of infringements of legal rights.

Other laws of general application that play some role in the foreign business environment in China include the PRC Constitution, which sets forth the basic organization of the state and specifies various legal rights including principles for foreign investment;[44] regulations on land administration, which dictate fee schedules and policy requirements for transfers of land use rights;[45] and a myriad of public security measures that affect travel of foreign personnel.[46]

These laws of general application will not be addressed directly, but do play a role to some extent in each of the five substantive topic areas under discussion.

C. Administrative Reforms

An important aspect of legal reform in China that potentially affects all aspects of foreign economic relations concerns administrative reform. The conventional Chinese approach to administrative law emphasized a positivist effort to structure and empower bureaucratic organs, and to allocate authority among them. The focus was state-centric, emphasizing substantive authority, rather than procedural protections for the subjects of that authority. As a result, little emerged in the way of doctrinal support for the role of external controls over administrative conduct.

The struggle over the form and extent of bureaucratic reform was played out during the course of discussion and enactment of the Administrative Litigation Law of the PRC (ALL).[47] The ALL was part of a larger effort to make China's administrative bureaucracy more accountable, and formalized the authority of the People's Courts to review administrative agency decisions. Although the principle that administrative decisions could be appealed to the courts had been recognized previously in the context of specific regulatory areas such as taxation and Customs, the ALL extends the principle to a broader range of administrative decisions and provides procedural rules for appeals.

Under the ALL, foreign business enterprises may challenge the legality of decisions by Chinese administrative organs. Although only the administrative organizations themselves may be defendants under the ALL,[48] the cause of action may arise as a result of an individual official's act.[49] The ALL does not authorize the courts to review decisions by Communist Party organs, but it does authorize judicial review of administrative decisions of virtually all Chinese state agencies, both central and local.

The types of bureaucratic decisions subject to judicial review under the law fall into several categories of administrative conduct, many of which have significance for foreign businesses.[50] These include administrative decisions imposing fines; restricting or infringing on property rights; intervening in business operations; denying licenses; and a number of other matters.[51] The scope of administrative decisions subject to review under the ALL permits foreign businesses (as well as their domestic counterparts) to seek judicial review of a wide range of regulatory decisions. In addition, the ALL may permit challenges against administrative agencies to be filed as a result of individual officials abusing their official powers to elicit graft from business enterprises.

In contrast to these merits, however, stands the fundamental problem that the ALL does not permit review of discretionary decisions lawfully conferred on administrative agencies. In light of the textual ambiguities of Chinese laws and regulations, discretionary decisions are widespread and abuses of discretion are common. Nonetheless, these are outside the scope of ALL review. In addition, ALL review does not extend to the lawfulness of administrative regulations themselves: Administrative agencies can in effect legislate their own immunities from ALL review.[52] Despite these problems, however, the ALL does provide at least the beginnings of a system of judicial review by which foreign businesses can challenge abusive regulatory conduct.

D. External Influences

In addition to the effects of domestic policy changes, the Chinese foreign business regime is affected by international influences. China's application to resume membership in the GATT and the scrutiny that this has engendered have played an important role in encouraging China to reform many of its trade, investment, and finance systems.[53] Other external influences have included bilateral relationships that have yielded additional efforts at reforming various aspects of China's foreign business regime. The U.S.–China Market Access Agreement, for example, called for elimination of quotas on imports, elimination of import substitution, and increased transparency in commodity inspection.[54] Several memoranda of understanding between China and the United States have had a significant impact on China's intellectual property protection system.[55] Finally, increased business ties with Europe,[56] and with Taiwan, Singapore, and other overseas Chinese communities[57] represent yet another source of foreign influence on China's approaches to managing its foreign economic relations.

Although these channels for foreign influence on China's regulatory systems have major long-term significance, their impact in the short term is likely to be limited. Promises of regulatory reform in response to foreign pressure have often been subverted by parochial policy priorities. For example, in response to criticisms by GATT members that China's commodity inspection system permitted non-tariff barriers, government statements were made to the effect that the system would be disbanded. However, it was widely suspected among foreign business operators in Beijing that the activities of the Commodity Inspection Administration would continue on an informal level (primarily in the context of customer acceptance of goods) and under a differently named organization, although the purposes and personnel would remain the same. Another example concerns the elimination of import quotas, where restrictions with equal or greater effect remain in place through limits on foreign exchange spending. Finally, the Chinese agreement in 1989 to improve its intellectual property protection system was so ineffectual that the U.S. Trade Representative (USTR) was compelled to bring yet another round of pressure to bear in 1992 and again in 1994. Nonetheless, among the generic factors affecting the role of law in China's foreign economic relations, foreign influences cannot be ignored.

* * *

The issues of basic philosophies, laws of general application, administrative review, and foreign influences each affect the content and performance of the legal regimes for China's foreign economic relations. They should be borne in mind in reviewing the substantive discussions that follow.

CHAPTER 2

Foreign Trade

I. The Legal Regime Governing China's Foreign Trade System

The legal regime governing China's foreign trade relations is organizationally disparate and substantively driven by policy concerns. Prior to the enactment of a unified Foreign Trade Law in June 1994,[1] Chinese foreign trade relations were governed by a variety of specific laws and regulations governing different aspects of the system, often with little or no attempt at consistency. This approach continues even after the enactment of the Foreign Trade Law, and as a result, China's foreign trade system is best viewed in the context of its organizational structure and operational aspects. This discussion will focus on the institutional structure of the Ministry in Charge; the trade licensing system; the commodity inspection system; and the system for customs and tariffs.

The reforms in China's trade system since 1978 have been dramatic.[2] The most important changes have occurred in the institutional structure involving the Ministry in Charge and its affiliated units. These in turn have affected the role of trade licensing. Efforts to augment the licensing system were evident in the establishment of the import and export commodity inspection systems. The Customs Service plays a critical role in enforcing licensing and commodity inspection requirements, and in administering trade tariffs. These four components remain critical to China's foreign trade system generally, although their character and effects have varied over time and in response to specific circumstances—notably China's campaign to gain accession to the GATT and the World Trade Organization (WTO). This discussion of the role of law in China's foreign trade will focus on the legal regime governing foreign trade, the performance of the four aspects of the legal regime, and the range of attitudes that help to explain performance.

A. Institutional Structure: The Ministry in Charge and the National Foreign Trade Corporations

The formation of the Ministry of Foreign Economic Relations and Trade (MOFERT) in 1982 heralded a major change in the institutional structure of China's foreign trade system.[3] The former Ministries of Foreign Trade and Foreign Economic Relations were combined with the State Commissions on Foreign Investment and Imports & Exports to form the new megaministry. This indicated an effort to coordinate trade policy with other aspects of China's foreign economic relations. MOFERT was initially given authority to supervise the conduct of foreign trade by Chinese enterprises. Among MOFERT's internal departments were the import and export administrations, which oversaw such matters as licensing and the approval of trade contracts. The recent renaming of the MOFERT as Ministry of Foreign Trade and Economic Cooperation (MOFTEC) has little to do with foreign trade issues but is indicative of changing policies toward foreign investment.

Beginning in the 1950s, China's foreign trade was in the main conducted by national foreign trade corporations (NFTCs) organized under MOFERT or under its provincial or local commissions and bureaus. These NFTCs had a near monopoly on the conduct of foreign trade.[4] Under this system, the local branches of the NFTCs were subject to supervision both by local government authorities and also by the head office in Beijing. Gradually, in response primarily to domestic political pressures, other companies were granted the authority to conduct foreign trade, and the monopoly enjoyed by the MOFERT NFTCs was eroded significantly. An important aspect of trade reform recently has been the further decentralization of the state trading apparatus and the expanded grants of trading authority to Chinese firms that are not part of the MOFERT/MOFTEC hierarchy.[5] Nonetheless, for much of the 1980s, most of China's foreign trade was conducted through the central and local-level NFTCs.

In 1988, China worked to decentralize its state trading corporations by establishing the former provincial branches of the NFTCs as separate corporations. In practice, however, the relationship between the former branches and their former central offices remained close, and fell far short of the arms-length relationship normally expected between subsidiary and parent. Chinese reference materials continued to refer to the newly incorporated provincial trading companies as branches (*fen gongsi*).[6] The guiding ideology underlying the decentralization effort was described as one that extolled "internal activities and external unification" (*nei huo wai tong*), a concept explained as meaning that foreign trade enterprises would have more autonomy to run their own internal production activities, while still operating within a unified government trading system.[7] Despite the decentralization effort, the managerial structure of Chinese foreign trade enterprises remained part of a larger system that emphasized collectivity and interrelatedness, and retained the vertical integration between the central foreign trade corporations and their subordinate foreign trade enterprises.[8]

As a result, producers of exports and the end users of imports were not directly involved in the commercial relationship with foreign business partners, although these ancillary units were involved in determining technical terms. The trade contracts signed by foreign businesses often did not include the Chinese enterprise that ultimately would produce or consume the traded items. Until recently, the local Chinese unit also bore little or no responsibility for profit and loss on the transaction. Moreover, the provincial trading companies generally lacked the authority to conclude business transactions on their own authority, but required at the very least informal and in many cases formal approval from higher levels before being permitted to conclude contracts. This has begun to change with the establishment of an agency trading system in which the NFTC acts only as a conduit for a service fee and the Chinese producer or consumer bears the commercial risk of the transaction.[9]

B. Trade Licensing and the State Plan

The administration of foreign trade by the Ministry in Charge was traditionally subject to the requirements of the state plan. The state foreign trade plan was approved by the State Planning Commission and relayed to the Ministry in Charge for dissemination to the NFTCs, from whence it would be sent down to the NFTC branches for concrete implementation in conjunction with the implementation work of the provincial and municipal foreign trade bureaus.[10] The Ministry in Charge would implement the state plan through the mechanisms of import and export licensing.[11] Foreign investment enterprises were subject to the same requirements, although in 1986, certain preferences were made available for them to permit foreign exchange balancing.[12]

Pursuant to the various trade licensing regulations,[13] the basic authority to issue trade licenses rested with the Ministry in Charge. The NFTCs generally received blanket approval to conduct foreign trade within their respective scopes of business, and subject to the requirements of the state plan. These enterprises were treated as having been issued general import and export licenses, and their trading activities were regulated primarily through Ministry directives rather than specific licensing decisions. Other enterprises were required to obtain specific import or export licenses, which varied in content and duration.

Information on the items subject to licensing, the duration of licenses, and other conditions was provided by the Ministry in Charge based on the requirements of the state plan.[14] However, despite the general directives of the state plan and the resulting MOFERT directives on licensing, the system was subject to extreme variation in the wake of changes in Chinese trade policies.

The effort to control the flow of imports and exports through the trade licensing system reflected several purposes. The first was the need to control foreign exchange by maximizing exports and limiting imports.[15] Also, trade licensing was geared toward coordinating access to goods for Chinese importers and coordinating market access strategies for Chinese exporters. Finally, the system operated as a powerful political tool of patronage, which dispensed access to foreign goods (for importers) and foreign exchange (for exporters) so as to maximize the political capital of the licensing organs.

In keeping with the Party's decision to reduce and gradually replace the formal role of the state plan with a series of policy directives,[16] it is expected that MOFTEC decision making on import–export matters will no longer have a direct planning component. Instead, state policies will dictate matters of import and export licensing and other aspects of the trade regime. In practice, because of the effects of instrumentalism and mercantilism to be discussed in this chapter, the end result is likely to be not much different than was the system under the state planning regime. Under the new Trade Law, the state retains the authority to control imports and exports through a licensing system.[17] Although the formal role of state planning has been replaced by references to state policies, trade licensing will continue to affect the identity and behavior of Chinese importers and exporters.

C. Commodity Inspection

The commodity inspection system was originally established in China during the 1950s, but after a significant period of inaction it was revitalized in 1984.[18] Commodity inspection is aimed at ensuring that products imported to China meet technical standards for health and safety, while also ensuring that exports meet the quality standards required by foreign consumers. However, as indicated by its use in Japan and Taiwan, the commodity inspection system is also a potential source of non-tariff barriers.

The commodity inspection system is administered by the PRC State Administration for Inspection of Import and Export Goods. As an organ separate from the Ministry in Charge, the Goods Inspection Administration diversifies the mechanisms for control over trade activities. This organ issues periodic lists of items that are subject to inspection, as well as publicizing the standards to be used.[19] Certificates confirming that the trade goods passed the inspection are required for passage through Customs. Whereas in the case of fungible goods like wheat or logs, an inspection of one lot within a shipment is usually sufficient, more rigorous inspections may be required of nonfungibles such as equipment and machinery.

The Chinese commodity inspection system represents a tension-ridden effort. On the one hand it is aimed apparently at legitimate goals of protecting domestic health and safety. On the other hand, the system is also subject to abuse in efforts to restrict trade.

D. Customs and Tariffs

Enforcement of licensing requirements, commodity inspection, and tariff schedules rests within the authority of the PRC Customs Administration.[20] Approval to clear goods for entry and exit is issued by Customs based on a review of the relevant export or import license. The Customs Service also ensures that commodity inspection certificates are in order before clearing goods for export or import.

In addition, the Customs Service administers the tariff system. Tariffs are imposed based on a schedule of goods and tariff rates. These schedules change periodically, but are easily obtained. However, the tariff rates are specified only as minimum and average rates, and no ceiling is formally imposed. As a result tariff amounts are not subject to clear limits, and are particularly amenable to adjustment in response to changes in Chinese import policies.

E. Update: The New Foreign Trade Law

In May 1994, the PRC enacted a comprehensive Trade Law.[21] Although intended in part to meet concerns of China's trading partners over issues of regulatory transparency, and part of a broader effort to pave the way for China's entry into the GATT and the World Trade Organization, the law's actual effects cannot be ascertained as yet. In general, the new law aims to clarify the status of decentralization in China's foreign trade companies. Yet the new legislation also affirms China's right to restrict imports and exports in pursuit of national policy goals. Until a pattern of implementation and practice emerges, it is premature to suggest which changes if any will be brought about by the enactment of the new law.

II. Performance of the Foreign Trade System

Foreign trade has contributed generally to China's economic growth. The total value of Chinese foreign trade has expanded from U.S.$21 billion in 1978 to

U.S.$166 billion in 1992 (averaging 15 percent per year in growth).[22] Exports grew from U.S.$10 billion in 1978 to over U.S.$80 billion in 1992 (16 percent annual growth), while imports grew from U.S.$11.1 billion in 1978 to U.S.$80 billion in 1992 (14 percent annual growth).[23] In 1993, export value grew to U.S.$91.8 billion, while the value of imports was U.S.$104 billion.[24] Although questions have been raised over China's 1993 trade deficit,[25] the general pattern has been one of steady growth in foreign trade generally. This impressive record notwithstanding, questions remain as to whether this impressive performance has occurred due to or in spite of the Chinese trade regime. The performance of the Chinese trading regime has reflected several distinct characteristics. Domestically, policy indeterminacy stemming from the politicization of trade policy has had an impact on the legal framework, while foreign forces have also played a role in influencing the performance of the system.

A. Policy Indeterminacy

Policy swings have impeded stability and prediction in the Chinese foreign trade system. Because of the bureaucratic nature of the state planned economy, responses to market changes are often too slow to be effective. By the time a political consensus permitting policy change has emerged, the market changes that are the focus of policy response are often well entrenched and not susceptible to quick adjustment. Also the severity of the policy response often outweighs the problem it was intended to address. For example, during late 1988 in the face of a severe foreign exchange imbalance, import licenses were severely restricted. This contributed to the rising price of consumer goods, which in turn exacerbated the popular discontent that led up to the Tiananmen crisis of 1989.[26]

Policy indeterminacy is also a result of the bureaucratic politics that characterize much of the government's decision making. Although the Ministry in Charge is responsible for coordinating trade policy and regulation, central and local bureaucracies have significant opportunities for input. Moreover, government departments outside of the Ministry in Charge have authority to issue rules within their scope of authority. Regulations on matters such as technical specification, packaging, transport methods, import substitution, and other activities are routinely issued by competing bureaucracies without proper consultation from the Ministry. For example, the Customs Administration repeatedly issues tariff schedules whose definitions and categories of products have a significant impact on valuation in the calculation of duties. These can have a significant effect on the flow of imports, regardless of how liberal or restrictive the Ministry's licensing policies are at the moment.

Ideological differences also play a role. China's opening to the outside world has not been without its critics. Some within the leadership have portrayed the reform policies as unnecessary and harmful concessions to the West.[27] Many of the reforms have been associated in the public mind with unwelcome socio-economic changes such as rising prices, increased disparities of wealth, declines in state services, rising crime, and other perceived ills, which are often attributed to China's "open door" policies of accommodating the needs of international trade and investment.[28] As well, political conflict plays a role, such as when the policy against issuing confirmed letters of credit in trade transactions appeared to be lifted briefly (and informally) following the Tiananmen fiasco, but was reimposed when a semblance of normalcy returned.

Organizational interests also have an effect on policy indeterminacy—particularly when combined with the political and commercial interests of Chinese organs that compete with or for imports. Despite the proliferation of trading companies in the emerging private sector, the vast majority of trading companies are affiliated, formally or otherwise, with government departments and ministries. For example, the electronics trading companies that were the product of downsizing of the Ministry of Machinery and Electronics Industry under Zou Jiahua retained their informal ties with that ministry, such that the company general managers were often recruited from their positions as bureau and section chiefs within the ministry. The role of organizational and commercial interests is also evident in the high tariffs on imports that directly compete with Chinese products—such as automobiles and computers. Increased commercialization in China may also give rise to new barriers to open trade, as local protectionism works to close markets.

One manifestation of policy indeterminacy concerns the phenomenon of decentralization and recentralization that has characterized trade policy for much of the first fifteen years of reform. Depending on a variety of factors, such as the condition of China's foreign exchange reserves and the general state of cooperation between the localities and the central government, provincial and local government authorities may be granted wide leeway to approve trade contracts and issue import and export licenses. Or they may be closely restricted. Although the financial conditions that motivate these changes are generally recognizable, in many instances the motivating factors are not so clear. This leads to a situation where foreign trading partners are unsure of the authority of local companies and government departments to conclude and approve contracts and trade licenses.

B. Legal Implications of Policy Indeterminacy

The indeterminacy that affects Chinese trade policy affects the interpretation of regulations significantly. As indicated in the Foreign Economic Contract Law, trade contracts must be in compliance with state policies, as these represent official articulation of the public interest.[29] Similarly, the Customs Law and the regulations on import and export licensing refer specifically to the need for policy control.[30] This permits approval authorities (whose consent is generally a condition for legal validity)[31] wide discretion in approving trade transactions.

Implementing officials also refer to policy routinely in making their decisions. For example, during 1988–89, officials at MOFERT and its subordinate NFTCs explained the denial of export licenses for local shippers by reference to internal policies restricting to a few selected central-level organs the right to export silk and cashmere. Commodity inspection decisions are also governed by transitory policies.[32] Although couched in terms of environmental and consumer protection, the import inspection system is widely believed to be the source of non-tariff barriers used to restrict imports in specifically identified sectors of the Chinese economy.[33]

* * *

In sum, the performance of the Chinese trade regime has been impressive in the area of growth, but less so in the area of law. The indeterminacy of policy and the effects of a changing international environment have made the legal and regulatory regime unpredictable. Although China's foreign trade efforts have been generally successful in generating trade surpluses,[34] the PRC experienced a trade deficit in 1993 and may well do so again in 1994. Despite the positive expansion of trade on the whole, it remains uncertain whether this will continue to benefit China. China's ability to manage its trade relations will require greater consistency in trade policy and law.

III. Attitudes Affecting Performance of the System

Among the factors that affect China's foreign trade regime are official attitudes that inform the behavior of the system. Two factors predominate Chinese official attitudes toward the role of law in trade matters, namely, instrumentalism and mercantilism. These are mutually reinforcing attributes that have a significant effect on the operation of the foreign trade system, and on the prospects for changes in the future.

The instrumentalism of Chinese legal approaches to foreign trade is evident in the statements of purpose that accompany virtually all laws and regulations in the area. In the area of licensing regulations and customs administration, applicable rules are heavily weighted toward the pursuit of policy goals. Indeed, legal reform generally is presented as an expression of policy changes designed to reform the Chinese economy.[35] China's initial response to inquiries about its economy from GATT members also reveals this approach, suggesting that changes had taken place in the Chinese economy as a result of laws enacted to bring about such change.[36] Aside from the formalism inherent in assuming that enacted law will bring about the desired results, such statements reveal the purposes to which law is put: Law is intended not to express principles of general applicability or specific rules consistent with principles applicable in other spheres of life, but rather to achieve particular and often narrow policy goals.

The instrumentalism of the Chinese trade law regime takes on greater importance when combined with the mercantilism of underlying policies. Generally speaking, mercantilism entails the use of the regulatory resources of the nation-state explicitly in pursuit of national economic interests.[37] Attention has been called to the mercantilism of Chinese trade policy, particularly in the areas of foreign exchange policy and the role of Special Economic Zones.[38] Yet another example may be found in China's response to the North America Free Trade Agreement, which has been less than enthusiastic. Official indicators of Chinese government policy have contained reservations about NAFTA as an expression of trade protectionism.[39] Unofficial contacts have expressed doubts about NAFTA as well.[40] The consistency evident among Chinese views on NAFTA reveals the extent of apprehension and uncertainty about the goals and consequences of NAFTA. Coming on the heels of renewed efforts to establish a unified European market and the possibility of the establishment of a trading bloc among the Association of Southeast Asian Nations (ASEAN), NAFTA is perceived in China as evidence that Western countries are willing to impose requirements aimed at forcing China's foreign trade and investment to be more open, while also being willing to close their own markets to Chinese exports. This double standard is particularly poignant for the Chinese because the formal signing of NAFTA in December 1992 came shortly after the conclusion of the U.S.–China Market Access Agreement in October 1992.[41]

Yet as currently formulated, the NAFTA agreement does not appear likely to have a significant direct impact on China's economic relations with North America under current policies.[42] China's capacity to adjust its export policies in order to adapt to changing conditions in the world market suggests that comparative advantage will permit it to weather whatever direct effects NAFTA's terms engender for Chinese exports to North America. On the investment side, China's capital export policies and its attraction as a target for investment have little to do with the investment preferences conferred by NAFTA. The extent to which NAFTA affects Chinese trade and investment relations will depend in large part on China's own foreign economic policies—such that adaptation to market changes and accession to mutually beneficial trade and investment agreements may diminish or erase NAFTA's immediate and long-term effects.

Chinese apprehensions about NAFTA reveal much about Chinese assumptions about the role of law in protecting the national economic interests of states, and also suggest that concessionary approaches to its trading partners may not be easily forthcoming. Although the Chinese government's view that NAFTA exemplifies the indeterminacy of law and its subservience to the economic interests of states may find some support in the doctrines of orthodox Marxism, it tends to ignore the underlying assumptions that inform GATT doctrine. Based on notions about market autonomy within a framework of general legal principles for international trade, GATT permits the establishment of free trade zones because such economic alliances that maximize efficiencies will ultimately benefit the system as a whole.[43] The expectation that NAFTA will unavoidably hurt Chinese economic ties with North America also suggests that the avenues for avoiding these effects through the negotiation or amendment of bilateral agreements that reduce Chinese trade barriers have not seriously been considered. The Chinese interpretation of NAFTA as a threat to China's world trade relations reveals instrumentalist assumptions about the use of law to maximize economic advantage.

IV. Implications

The role of instrumentalism and mercantilism in China's foreign trade has several implications. First, the emphasis on instrumentalism may inhibit the emergence of a predictable trade regime. Policy responses to changing conditions are naturally part of any country's trade system. But the existence of underlying principles is essential to basic stability and predictability. If these are lost in the pursuit of mercantilist expediency, policy may well become less predictable. Under such circumstances, foreign corporations engaged in trade with China may increasingly be hesitant to expand their trade relations with China. Foreign governments may also be deterred from increasing their support for trade with China if the legal regime supporting such trade lacks basic predictability and stability.

Second and potentially more serious is the potential that China's own instrumentalist and mercantilist approaches to the role of law in foreign trade may cause it to misinterpret trade policies of other nations. Obviously self-interest plays a role in every country's trade policy, but self-interest may include policies favoring sustainable development in the Third World, environmental responsibility, or other objectives that may not be susceptible to understanding when viewed purely from a standpoint of mercantilist instrumentalism. The potential for Chinese misunderstanding of the policies and behavior of other countries may also lead to counterproductive efforts—such as the North East Asia trading bloc raised as a potential response to NAFTA—that may work to the detriment of all. While China's participation in GATT and the World Trade Organization may well militate against many of the mercantilist policies of the past, this too will require fundamental changes in policies and attitudes.

CHAPTER 3

Foreign Investment

I. The Legal Regime for Foreign Investment in China

The legal regime governing foreign investment activities in China was established following the Third Plenum of the Eleventh Central Committee in December 1978, when China announced the "open door" policy intended to attract foreign capital and technology. However the decision to open China's economy to foreign investment was tempered by a desire to control the foreign presence in order to prevent disruptions to its socialist society. The legal regime for foreign investment reflects these tensions.

A. Foreign Investment Enterprises

The Chinese government has permitted the direct investment of foreign capital through several business forms, including equity joint ventures, cooperative joint ventures, wholly foreign-owned joint ventures, and natural resource development projects. Initially these forms were differentiated fairly strictly, but in recent years the distinctions have gradually begun to fade.

Equity Joint Ventures

The legal framework for equity joint ventures (EJVs) is set forth mainly in the Joint Venture Law and the Joint Venture Law Implementing Regulations.[1] The Chinese government initially considered EJVs to be the preferred means of introducing foreign investment into the country, because it was believed such investment vehicles would quicken the flow of technology and management skills into Chinese hands. Therefore, steps were taken to codify the legal status of EJVs in advance of other forms of investment vehicles.[2] The Joint Venture Law provides but a brief (fifteen articles) collection of legislative instructions for equity joint ventures, although at the time of its issuance the Joint Venture

22

Law offered a degree of security to foreign investors by guaranteeing their right to invest and earn a profit in China. The promulgation of the Joint Venture Law Implementing Regulations was an effort to induce greater confidence in the foreign investor community. The Implementing Regulations addressed a variety of critical issues, including profit repatriation, technology transfer, labor, land use, and foreign exchange. Prior to enactment of the Implementing Regulations, these issues were dealt with through contract terms often imposed by government authorities. However, the four-year delay in enacting the Implementing Regulations, combined with their still-cursory form, were emblematic of potential problems with Chinese legislative and regulatory efforts—policy uncertainty and bureaucratic inaction would stand as continuing barriers to the effective use of law to regulate foreign economic relations.

An equity joint venture is a limited liability business association involving Chinese and foreign parties and is regarded as a legal person and a distinct taxable entity. The liability of each party is limited to the extent of its capital contribution. All EJV participants share profits and losses based on their registered capital contributions. Although the foreign side must contribute at least one quarter of the registered capital, there is no upper limit to its capital contribution.[3] Foreign partners generally are expected to contribute foreign exchange and advanced technology, equipment, materials, and industrial property, whereas the Chinese side may provide land use rights, buildings, and equipment. The Chinese side seldom contributes cash as part of its equity contribution. Equity participation is evidenced by an "investment certificate" issued by the joint venture.[4] Investment certificates are not freely negotiable and may be transferred only after obtaining the consent of the other EJV participant(s).

The Board of Directors is the highest organ of authority of an EJV and is responsible for deciding all major issues concerning operation, management, and organic changes.[5] The Board must have a minimum of three directors, who are appointed by the equity participants. Originally, the Chair was to be appointed by the Chinese side. With the enactment of 1990 revisions to the Joint Venture Law, the Chair may be appointed by either side, while the Vice Chair is then appointed by the side that has not selected the Chair.[6] The general manager and deputy general managers, who may be either Chinese or foreigners, are appointed by the board and are responsible for the routine management tasks.[7]

To establish an EJV, the participants must first obtain preliminary approval from the relevant department overseeing the project. This requires the Chinese side to prepare and submit a preliminary feasibility study and project proposal. Upon obtaining preliminary approval, the Chinese side is permitted to engage in detailed negotiations with its foreign counterpart. It is at this second stage that the parties need to prepare a formal feasibility study, which is distributed to government units overseeing the critical aspects of the project such as utility and transportation demands, factor inputs, labor requirements, funding and foreign exchange needs, and product prices. This step ensures that the venture project comports with state plans and policies. After the formal feasibility study is reviewed by the State Planning Commission, the Ministry in Charge (MOFTEC, formerly MOFERT) authorizes the parties to prepare the joint venture contract and articles of association.[8] These documents must be approved by MOFTEC prior to the issuance of a certificate of approval. Once such approval is obtained the parties may sign the EJV contract and obtain a business operation license from the local office of the State Administration of Industry and Commerce (SAIC).[9]

Cooperative Joint Ventures

Cooperative joint ventures (CJVs) are more flexible than equity joint ventures, and have a business structure somewhat akin to a strategic partnership. During the first decade of the open door policy, China dealt with CJVs by analogy to the regulations governing equity joint ventures. In the absence of specific governing regulations investors devised creative operating structures and management approaches. CJV participants determine the amount and type of capital to be contributed by each side, and the relative distribution of profits and losses. The sharing of profits and losses may differ from the capital contribution of the parties, and there is no 25 percent minimum equity contribution requirement for foreign investors. Unlike EJVs, foreign participants are permitted to recoup their capital investment prior to the expiration of the CJV.

It was not until mid-1988 that the Chinese government established a formal regulatory framework for CJVs with the enactment of Cooperative Enterprise Law.[10] Although this legislation approved many of the flexible characteristics that evolved for CJVs in practice, it did subject CJVs to a number of restrictions similar to those found in the Joint Venture Law. For example, the parties are required to form a joint management body responsible for deciding major issues similar to the Board of Directors for equity joint ventures.[11] In a manner similar to EJV procedures, the parties seeking to establish a CJV must obtain approval for a project feasibility study as a prelude to beginning negotiations.[12] Once concluded, the CJV contract, articles of association, and other relevant documents must be submitted to MOFTEC for examination and approval.[13] Once the certificate of approval is issued, the parties may then apply for a business license with SAIC: The CJV comes into existence when the business license is issued, and may apply to obtain status as a legal person.[14]

Wholly Foreign-Owned Enterprise

A wholly foreign-owned enterprise (WFOE) is a limited liability company established in China and owned solely by a foreign entity. Subject to Chinese regulatory requirements in such areas as labor relations and environmental protection, the foreign investor determines the management structure and procedures and bears responsibility for profits and losses.

Although the Chinese government initially did not actively encourage WFOEs, perhaps because of the perception that little technology or know-how would flow through such an entity, it did permit a small number of WFOEs to be established on an experimental basis in the Special Economic Zones (SEZs) during the early 1980s.[15] In April 1986 a law on wholly foreign-owned enterprises was promulgated in an effort to clarify the legal position of WFOEs.[16] Several factors contributed to the Chinese government's greater enthusiasm toward WFOEs, including the desire to introduce more foreign capital despite indicators of growing disenchantment among foreign investors with joint ventures. The WFOE Law sought to allay the fears of foreign investors in part through its provision that China would not nationalize or expropriate a WFOE, except under special circumstances in which case reasonable compensation would be made.[17]

The number of WFOEs remained small immediately after the enactment of the WFOE Law, although there was a gradual increase beginning in 1987 and 1988.[18] In December 1990 implementing regulations for the WFOE Law came into effect, providing greater detail as to the rights and obligations of WFOEs.[19] These regulations clarify operating conditions for WFOEs and indicate the industries (such as media, foreign trade, insurance, and telecommunications) in which WFOEs are prohibited[20] and those (public utilities, real estate, trust and investment, leasing, communications, and transportation) in which WFOEs are restricted and/or require special MOFTEC approval.[21]

Natural Resource Development Ventures

As their name implies, natural resource development ventures (NRDVs) are cooperative efforts to explore and develop mineral, petroleum, and other resources within China. Although the number of these ventures has been relatively small, they have accounted for a significant share of the total value of foreign investment due to the scale and capital intensiveness of such projects. The development of offshore oil resources is a typical example of where investment vehicles of this kind have been utilized.[22]

In a NRDV the foreign partner generally is responsible for the up-front capital expenditures during the resource exploration phase and most or all of the risk. During the second phase, the foreign and Chinese participants share in the capital investment and risk allotment. In the event that the parties determine that resources can be profitably extracted and marketed, production occurs, and profits are divided according to an agreed formula after costs and taxes are subtracted.

The structure of NRDVs is similar to cooperative joint ventures. This permits the parties to make flexible arrangements for the sharing of profits. Furthermore, as foreigners are prohibited from obtaining an ownership stake in the extracted resources, alternative means can be devised for remitting the profits of the foreign party. Recent policy decisions permit the NRDV approach to be used for onshore petroleum and mining projects.[23]

B. Foreign Representative Offices

The Chinese government does not include foreign representative offices within the classification of foreign investment enterprise (FIE). These offices are seen essentially as sales and liaison offices that do not represent channels for capital and technology entering China. Rather, they are viewed as vehicles for drawing foreign exchange out of China in the form of sales proceeds. Despite their exclusion from the Chinese classification of investments, representative offices often constitute a significant capital commitment on the part of the foreign investor, hence they are included here as a form of foreign investment.

The registration and operation of representative offices are governed by a series of regulations, the first of which was enacted in October 1980.[24] This measure requires all representative offices to apply for and obtain approval to establish a resident office prior to engaging in any business activities in China. In addition, there are a number of provisions that limit and monitor the permissible activities of the office and its staff. These include residency permits, banking and tax registration, customs matters, and employment of local personnel. A measure underscoring the close control of representative offices is the annual registration renewal requirement.

A resident representative office is a relatively low-risk means by which foreign businesses can establish a presence in China. Foreign companies are not required to deposit registered capital, although they must fund the expenses of setting up an office. The foreign party is not required to seek out a Chinese partner, although finding a Chinese sponsor is a prerequisite to obtaining approval to establish the representative office. Representative offices are prohibited from engaging in direct business operations, and instead are used primarily to facilitate trade contacts and promote sales and services, notably in the banking and financial sector.

In early 1983 China enacted regulations clarifying the role that could be played by the representative offices of foreign financial institutions.[25] These measures permitted foreign banks to establish representative offices to provide business liaison, consultation, information, and related services, but expressly prohibited them from engaging in "direct profit-making business activities," such as the granting of loans and handling of foreign exchange.[26] In addition to establishing registration requirements, the 1983 regulations set forth specific operating rules and designated Beijing, the SEZs, and certain other designated cities, such as Shanghai and Dalian, as the only permissible locations in which financial institutions could be based.

In June 1991 the People's Bank of China (PBOC) issued a new set of regulations that amplified the registration and reporting requirements of the representative offices of foreign financial institutions.[27] The 1991 Representative Office Regulations also eased the procedures for establishing branch offices and eliminated the restrictions on office staff size and geographical location.

The State Council's 1994 Regulations on Control of Foreign Banking Institutions now permit foreign banks to engage in a broader range of activities, including branches, joint venture banks, WFOE and JV finance companies, and even foreign banks headquartered in China (WFOEs).[28] Although this represents a significant opening of the finance market to foreign investment, restrictions remain. All activities of foreign banks must be denominated in foreign currency. Foreign banks are not permitted to extend their business operations to finance transactions involving local currency. As well, foreign finance activities remain subject to approval by the PBOC, which of course has a strong vested interest in protecting the market position of its own state banks and the Chinese banking system in general. As discussed in Chapter 5, the pending enactment of a Banking Law and a Central Bank Law may better illuminate some of these issues. Beginning in 1980, four special Economic Zones (SEZs) were established, three (Shenzhen, Shantou, Zhuhai) in Guangdong and one (Xiamen) in Fujian. These were soon followed by a fifth SEZ on Hainan Island, and Economic and Technology Development Zones (ETDZs) in most of the coastal cities.[29]

C. Foreign Investment Inducements

From the time it announced the open door policy, the Chinese government has actively tried to attract foreign investment. Recognizing the need for a secure business environment, Beijing undertook efforts to build up the legal system for foreign investment. The National People's Congress enacted a new Constitution in 1982 articulating the right of foreigners to invest in China and to have their investments protected by the laws of China.[30] The Joint Venture Implementing Regulations were enacted in 1983 and amended in 1986, further clarifying a number of important issues, such as profit repatriation. The Foreign Economic Contract Law (FECL) was enacted in 1985, followed by the General Principles of Civil Law in 1986, both of which set forth a number of basic legal rules with important application to foreign investments. By clarifying such concepts as "legal persons" the General Principles of Civil Law provided assistance to investors in identifying which organizations and entities had authority to enter into contracts or were acting within the scope of their authority. As well, China worked to conclude a series of bilateral investment treaties that might lend greater predictability to China's legal regime.[31]

Some of these efforts helped induce additional foreign investment: Record amounts of capital were committed to joint venture projects in 1984 and 1985.[32] The effects were not long-lasting, however, and by 1985 the rapid growth rates in pledged investment dropped off significantly and continued to drop through 1986.[33] Among the principal reasons for the rapid and sudden decline in investment was Beijing's tightening of access to foreign exchange in order to reduce import levels. This policy had an immediate negative effect on many, if not most, foreign investment ventures.[34]

The Chinese government responded to the investment decline and concerns of the investors with regulations aimed specifically at encouraging foreign investment. In October 1986 the Provisions of the State Council of the People's Republic of China for the Encouragement of Foreign Investment, popularly named the 22 Articles, were promulgated.[35] The 22 Articles addressed a number of bureaucratic problems facing many foreign investors. Among the inducements provided in the 22 Articles were the following:

1. Tax reductions for export enterprises and advanced technology enterprises;
2. Stabilized land use fees;
3. The promise of managerial autonomy;
4. Foreign exchange balancing measures;
5. Favorable treatment on import and export licenses;
6. Preferential treatment in bank loans, access to raw materials, and other areas.

Specific details on these and other incentives were subsequently spelled out in a series of implementing regulations enacted in late 1986 and early 1987.[36] Additional regulations were adopted by various provinces and localities, building on the precedent set by the 22 Articles.[37] Although the 22 Articles and its progeny were clearly aimed at favoring enterprises that would meet China's national policy goals of technology acquisition and export promotion,[38] and although there were many questions in the foreign business community over the practical effects of the regulations, as a whole they served as an important statement of

China's continued commitment to the use of incentives to attract foreign investment.

D. The Company Law of the PRC

In December 1993 the NPC promulgated the PRC Company Law, which formalizes the rules and procedures for company operations.[39] Based on a draft that had been submitted the previous March after undergoing years of refinement and debate, and drawing on existing texts in central and local regulations,[40] the Company Law went into effect on July 1, 1994. It includes 230 articles covering the establishment and organization of companies, bond issues, accounting matters, mergers, bankruptcy and liquidation, responsibilities of branches of foreign companies, and other matters. Of particular interest for the operation of foreign investment enterprises in China are the provisions on limited liability companies, which appear to have application to joint ventures and wholly foreign-owned enterprises. In addition, the Company Law contains provisions permitting foreign companies to establish branches in China, thus raising new possibilities for foreign investment. Implementing regulations and judicial and administrative rulings will likely clarify the application of this important new legislation to foreign investment activities in the PRC.

II. Performance of the Chinese Foreign Investment System

Over the first fifteen years of reform, foreign investment rates have increased steadily from an annual average of just over U.S.$2 billion during 1979–85 to over U.S.$ 6.3 billion in 1985 and again in 1988 and 1989.[41] During 1990 the value of foreign investment contracts was over $6.5 billion,[42] whereas in 1991 the figure was nearly $12 billion,[43] and in 1992 the total value of foreign investment contracts was $57.2 billion.[44] In 1993, the total contracted value was U.S.$122.7 billion.[45] Even when accounting for gaps between contracted values and funds actually committed,[46] there is little doubt that China has remained an attractive target for foreign capital. Although labor-intensive manufacturing remains the mainstay, the economic sectors in which foreign investment has been targeted have also diversified.[47]

On the other hand, the distribution of foreign investment has not been uniform, but rather has been concentrated in the South. During 1983–88, Guangdong and Fujian provinces received nearly half of all foreign investment in China.[48] Although the location of three out of the four original Special Economic Zones in Guangdong and the fourth in Fujian certainly contributed to this phenomenon early in the 1980s, the continued concentration of foreign investment in Guangdong suggests that other factors are at play. In particular, the role of familial ties between Guangdong and Hong Kong have played a significant role.[49] Also, the market-oriented supports—labor force, transportation, access to imported technologies, and so forth—that exist in South China are generally seen as superior to those available elsewhere.[50] Perhaps most important has been the commitment of the Guangdong provincial government to establishing a consistent policy of support for economic growth.[51] The ability of other urban regions, particularly Shanghai and the other coastal cities, to succeed in their efforts to duplicate Guangdong's success will likely depend as well on informal familial networks and local regulatory policies that are supportive of the conditions necessary for expanding investment.

The role that consistent and responsive policies linked to market conditions have played in Guangdong's successful experience in attracting foreign investment suggests that these policies may be critical to the success of China's overall foreign investment regime. Accordingly, the following discussion of the Chinese regulatory regime for foreign investment will give particular attention to the effects of policy changes and formalistic assessments of investment incentives.

A. Policy Indeterminacy

As with trade matters, the regulatory regime for foreign investment in China has been subject to significant fluctuations due to ongoing policy changes. During the nearly fifteen years since the Third Plenum of the Eleventh CPC Central Committee in December 1978, China's open door policy toward foreign investment has shifted between extremes of openness and restriction.[52] During the first few years after 1978, China's initial opening was greeted with great enthusiasm by foreign firms, who were then disappointed by subsequent retrenchment policies during which numerous foreign contracts were canceled and a sense of gloom descended on foreign business interests.

The Chinese government's renewed attention to attracting foreign business and the enactment of additional regulations on joint ventures and tax matters spurred greater optimism and activity in the mid-1980s. However, foreign business people were continually frustrated by the inadequacy of the regulatory regime, the impenetrability of the Chinese bureaucracy, and a multitude of practical obstacles. The State Council's 1986 "Measures for the Encouragement of Foreign Investment" (the so-called 22 Articles) offered the prospect of further improvements, but these appeared doomed by the Tiananmen massacre and the nationwide repression that followed. Deng Xiaoping's 1992 visit to Shenzhen and his speeches extolling the virtues of establishing a socialist market economy in China brought yet another wave of foreign business interest. The seemingly endless policy oscillations since 1978 have made it difficult if not impossible for foreign investors to reach firm conclusions about governing policy.

The cycle of reform, overheating, and retrenchment was repeated when Vice Premier Zhu Rongji took charge in 1993 of a vigorous effort to rein in an overheated economy.[53] Although there was wide agreement among Chinese economists and foreign businesses that the campaign was necessary, there were major concerns that it would not be successful because of the capacity of local officials to resist central policies. The success of Shanghai, Sichuan, Guangdong, and other regions in obtaining exemptions signaled the limitations of effectuating the retrenchment policy. Nonetheless, the campaign certainly had the potential to affect foreign investment activities. Although the financial restructuring campaign did not target foreign contracts specifically, this must be viewed in light of two major limitations.

First, the contracts excluded from the retrenchment were those that had already been formally approved, and did not include agreements, letters of intent, and other informal agreements, which under the Foreign Economic Contract Law must still be formally approved in order to be legally valid.[54] Although these kinds of agreements might well rise to the status of contract under American rules of contract law, they are not treated as formal binding contracts under Chinese law. Thus, the retrenchment efforts had the potential to affect many agreements between foreign and Chinese parties, notwithstanding official implications to the contrary. Moreover, Zhu's campaign complicated the process of ensuring that both local- and central-level approvals are in place for particular investment projects.

Second, the real effect of Zhu's campaign was to control the availability of credit at the local level, with several likely effects on foreign investment. The credit crunch restricted the ability of local enterprises to invest in physical plants that then would be used as local contribution in joint venture enterprises with foreign businesses. Also, the restrictions worked to restrict funds available to Chinese enterprises for buying products produced by foreign investment enterprises. Finally, the economic pressures generated by the restrictions affected the cost of business operations for foreign investment enterprises and local enterprises alike.

In addition to changes in central policies, policy indeterminacy is exacerbated by local officials who often employ their discretion in policy implementation to pursue local parochial interests. Inconsistent policy decisions are often the product of the conflicting goals of different bureaucracies, whose regulatory power is subject to few effective limits. For example, provisions of the People's Bank of China prohibiting foreign bank representative offices from engaging in profit-making activities were contradicted by the practice of local tax officials

who imposed foreign enterprise income taxes on such offices based on calculations of "deemed profits."[55] As well, national regulations are subject to
countermanding by local measures. For example, the State Council's Measures
for Encouraging Foreign Investment included a specific provision granting foreign investment enterprises autonomy in hiring and firing staff without interference. Yet this was quickly contradicted by local regulations requiring labor
union approval for personnel dismissals—in effect imposing the requirement of
Party approval for such decisions.[56] Local authorities have also been known to
exceed their authority in unlawfully dismissing joint venture managerial personnel.[57] Differing patterns of regulatory intervention have also been evident, such
that in some regions administrative agencies have been quick to impose amendments to joint venture contracts in order to resolve disagreements, whereas in
others regulatory inaction has been the norm.[58]

The effects of varying Chinese economic policies on foreign investment over
the past ten or more years have been quite substantial. Indeed it is the primacy
given to policy over regulatory content that compounds the problem. The principles and standards set down in formal laws and regulations are constantly
altered to comply with changing policy pronouncements. In this constantly
changing policy environment, it is not surprising that foreign investors find
prediction and certainty difficult.[59] Indeed, the retrenchment initiated in 1993
has largely been curtailed—to the relief of foreign firms, but also as further
evidence of continuing policy oscillation.[60] The inherent difficulties of predicting market changes are compounded by difficulties in predicting Chinese
bureaucratic behavior.

B. Formalism in Investment Incentives

In addition to the effects of policy changes there has been the problem of
overly formalistic approaches to investment incentives. The Chinese regulatory
regime places great emphasis on material inducements such as tax incentives to
increase foreign investment activity. Two examples are noteworthy: the regulation on tax reductions for foreign investment enterprises in the Special
Economic Zones and the 14 Coastal Cities,[61] and the State Council's 22 Articles investment incentive package of 1986. The tax reduction regulations provided a range of inducements for foreign investment enterprises in specific
manufacturing sectors. The 22 Articles provided for reduced taxes, fees, and
other costs across a broader spectrum.

Although the investment inducement provisions have been criticized on
grounds of ambiguity[62] and general inadequacy,[63] the most severe critique is
that they fail to address matters of primary concern to foreign business.[64] Foreign business objectives in China vary widely, but may be characterized gener-

ally as being centered on issues of access to information and management of risk. Each of these is critical to cost control and long-term operations. In the case of foreign businesses operating in China, access to information is of primary concern, as many firms' primary goals in China focus on positioning themselves for long-term access to the Chinese domestic market. Risk management is also important. Of course profits are a concern where foreign investment enterprises are already selling to the domestic market, but even though many firms wish to limit the costs of this exercise, short-term profit is not always an overriding consideration.

The goals of foreign businesses concerning risk and information require a modicum of predictability and transparency in Chinese laws and regulations and in the policies that inform them. Even though the Chinese government has evidenced a willingness to try to respond to the perceived concerns of foreign investors through the 22 Articles and the tax regulations on SEZs and Coastal Cities, the issues of risk and information were not addressed effectively. Problems with information transfer have been particularly evident in the use of "internal" (*neibu*) regulations, which are not available to foreigners and which have a significant bearing on the approval processes and subsequent regulation of enterprise activities. Although the use of internal regulations applying to foreign investment enterprises has declined since 1987 in response to MOFERT/MOFTEC directives, they remain an important yet invisible component of the regulatory system. Foreign investors face the quandary of being told that regulations prohibit certain activities, but then being refused access to those regulations.

Obstacles to receipt of information have extended to Chinese government departments, many of which—particularly at lower levels—are not fully or accurately apprised of changing government policies and regulations. For example, the implementing regulations that followed the 22 Articles were often not communicated effectively to provincial and county-level foreign investment and trade commissions and bureaus, to the detriment of foreign investors who tried to utilize these provisions at the local level.

In the policy-dominated environment of China's foreign investment regime, information about policy changes is particularly crucial. Yet this information also was not communicated to the foreign business community through formal channels, and so foreign investors were left to rely on their informal contacts to obtain information. Examples include the restrictions imposed in 1981-83[65] and again in the fall of 1988 as part of economic retrenchment policies, each of which had a significant impact on the operation of foreign investment enterprises and left them little or no opportunity to prepare.[66] As well, organizational changes in many government departments made it difficult for foreign business managers to contact relevant regulatory agencies. For example, personnel and organizational changes in the Foreign Investment Administration and Technology Import Administration of MOFERT/MOFTEC and within the State Administration for Industry and Commerce often have not been communicated fully to foreign businesses or their representatives in Beijing.

Risk management has been given cursory attention but little has been done that might have meaningful practical results. Thus, formalistic statements in the Wholly Foreign Owned Enterprise Law apparently limiting the government's ability to expropriate or nationalize foreign investment[67] were not persuasive in view of the obstacles to the conclusion of a foreign investment treaty with the United States that would address this issue in meaningful terms.[68]

Finally, investment inducement measures have paid little attention to infrastructural issues like energy, labor, transportation, and marketing. Issues such as transportation, communications, and energy tend to be addressed in China's own very long-term planning efforts, and are largely dependent on foreign programs. As exemplified by the transportation crises, telecommunications inadequacies, and routine energy shortages that plague all of China's major cities, little effort has been made in the near term to improve these conditions as they affect foreign investment enterprises. The general unwillingness of the Chinese government to issue sovereign guarantees for energy generation plants has contributed to delays in the application of foreign capital in this sector. Labor issues are only slowly being addressed, and despite efforts to free up unskilled labor markets in the cities, the market for skilled workers and professionals is very tightly restricted such that foreign enterprise employers must in effect "buy" their recruits from Chinese employers. The continuing role of the Foreign Enterprise Service Corporation (FESCO) in Beijing and its counterparts in other cities further restrains the autonomy of foreign businesses in the recruitment of staff. Although recent decisions permitting the use of foreign investment for retailing projects offer potential opportunities,[69] sales to the Chinese domestic market remain restricted, as indicated by the continued use of import substitution criteria and restrictions on retailing in domestic market sales.

* * *

Thus, the performance of the foreign investment system in China has been mixed. Steady inflows of capital have been matched by an ever-expanding array of laws and regulations aimed at foreign business activities. However, little attention has been paid to fundamental issues of policy dominance and indeterminacy, and regulatory formalism. Foreign investors face a regulatory environment that is unpredictable—both in the ever-changing content of central policy and in the discretionary decision making of local officials. At the same time, foreign investment also must comply with a formalistic and often unresponsive regulatory regime that assumes its own stability and effectiveness. Attempts to resolve these problems through bilateral treaties have not been altogether successful, as indicated by the difficulties facing U.S. and Canadian negotiations on BITs with China. The contradictions between the indeterminacy of the policy foundation and the rigidity of the regulatory form present significant obstacles to meaningful legal control over foreign business activities.

III. Attitudes Affecting Performance of the System

The characteristics of the Chinese foreign investment regime may be explained in part by reference to the attitudes in the Chinese leadership and among the system's administrators. The degree to which the system is vulnerable to policy changes reflects the instrumentalist nature of the Chinese legal system. Chinese laws and regulations on foreign investment represent a special set of rules aimed at achieving very specific goals. Investment activities are subordinated to policies of insularity intent on limiting the effects of foreign investment on the Chinese domestic economy. The most prominent example of this is the contract law system by which there are two separate laws, the ECL and the FECL, designed to regulate domestic and foreign contracts. This separation of the domestic (*guonei*) from the foreign-related (*shewai*) mirrors organization of most Chinese political organizations, which relegate the handling of foreigners to a special office—the so-called *waiban*—which often has little contact with the other activities of the institution.

This attitude of insularity affects the foreign investment system as well. Foreign investment rules were originally conceived of as necessary means to bring foreign capital to China, but were not indicative of the ways in which Chinese leaders wanted the domestic economy to run. For example, the Joint Venture Law made clear that these enterprises were seen as a limited and tightly controlled foray into foreign economic cooperation and were to be strictly segregated from the domestic economy.[70] The Joint Venture Law Implementing Regulations reveal additional attitudes about the limited scope for joint venture activities.[71] In view of these utilitarian approaches to the role of law in managing foreign investment, it is not surprising to find the rules heavily dependent on policy guidance. Yet, this creates significant obstacles to predictability and transparency in the regulatory process.

In order for utilitarian rules to be effective, they must be grounded in valid assumptions about the factors that motivate the behavior in question. The tendency of the Chinese regulatory effort to ignore market-oriented aspects of commercial decision-making by foreign firms reflects both lack of experience and ideological orientation. Simplistic Marxist assumptions about profit maximization distract decisionmakers from detailed inquiry into foreign firms' long-term goals concerning access to information and minimization of risk. Moreover, there has been an almost naive sense, born of formalistic assumptions about the effects of instrumentalist law, that the enactment of regulations can resolve and prevent problems. Thus, the 22 Articles were presented as effectively addressing the concerns of foreign business operators, whereas in fact they merely identified some of the problems and were largely ineffective in resolving them. Similarly, the regulations on import substitution were presented initially as a mechanism for resolving the problems of foreign exchange balancing, and later came to be used to prevent foreign investment firms from gaining entry into the domestic market. The problems of formalism are also evident in the general lack of attention to enforcement matters—such that enacting new regulations is often preferable to incurring the political cost of vigorous enforcement.

The instrumentalist and formalistic attitudes that inform much of the law and regulation that govern China's foreign investment regime are exacerbated by attitudes toward the flow of information. Obstacles to open transfer and receipt of information reflect both the parochialism of bureaucratic organizations in China as well as a political culture that does not consider openness to be a virtue. Regulatory authorities retain their political power in large part through the monopoly they hold on information and regulatory interpretation, and are as a result reluctant to permit this power to be weakened through the open dissemination of regulations and rules. Moreover, the political legitimacy of higher level organs often depends on the absence of outside challenges—such that higher levels do not welcome or tolerate debate from lower levels over matters of interpretation.

IV. Implications

The disparities between foreign investor priorities over information access and risk management, and the formalistic utilitarianism of the Chinese regulatory scheme have a range of implications. Although the possibility seems remote that foreign investors will lose interest in investing in China, continued increases in investment rates may be limited unless foreign businesses are given broader access to the domestic market. The ability of the Chinese government to protect its local industries against competition for better finances and more technologically advanced foreign investment enterprises may depend on establishing the conditions for China to operate as an efficient export platform in

East Asia. This will mean permitting foreign investors greater access to information, as well as greater attention to infrastructure matters, and a greater willingness to address issues of risk in a meaningful rather than formalistic way. Policy stability, and the resulting consistency in the regulatory regime will be essential. In the absence of efforts along these lines, China may well fail to live up to its potential to attract foreign investment.

CHAPTER 4

Technology Transfer

I. The Legal Regime for Technology Transfers to China

China's laws governing technology transfer have undergone significant changes between 1989 and 1993. These changes reflect an effort to accommodate conflicting foreign and domestic priorities. Conditions prior to 1989 set an important context for the reforms that have taken place during the past five years.

A. China's Technology Transfer Regime Prior to 1989

From 1949 through the late 1970s, China typically imported foreign technology through the wholesale purchase of integrated equipment or entire factories in an attempt to establish new enterprises and industries, particularly in the heavy industry sector.[1] China often was unable to absorb such technologies due to inadequate planning and infrastructure.[2] With the development of its open door policy after 1978, China adopted a new approach to technology transfer by emphasizing the use of technology to reform and upgrade existing enterprises.[3] As part of its drive to modernize its economy and simultaneously develop science and technology, China offered incentives to encourage the introduction of advanced technology. However, delays in legislation protecting intellectual property rights have hampered China's drive to obtain foreign advanced technologies.

During the first fifteen years of reform, two methods have stood out as the basis for transferring technology to China. The first approach involves a stand-alone licensing agreement by which the foreign technology owner agrees to transfer technology in exchange for a licensing fee or royalty payment. An alternative method is for a foreign enterprise to transfer technology as part of its capital contribution to a foreign investment enterprise (FIE: joint venture or a wholly foreign-owned enterprise). For economic and ideological reasons, China generally has not favored the expenditure of foreign exchange for the outright purchase of foreign technology.

Technology Transfer Legislation

Chinese technology transfer rules extend to both straight licensing agreements and to transfers of technology in the context of FIEs. Virtually all transfers of technology to China require contracts that, in addition to the general provisions of the Foreign Economic Contract Law, must meet specific requirements for technology contracts.

The basic requirements for technology transfer contracts involving foreign parties are set forth in the 1985 regulations on technology import contracts.[4] These established a broad definition of technology transfer to include not only the importation of patented equipment, but also transfers of technical services; know-how in the form of production design, processes, and management skills; and the assignment or licensing of industrial property rights. These regulations specify that imported technology must be "advanced and appropriate," which means that the technology be efficient, conducive to the development of new products, and capable of expanding exports.[5] A more detailed set of rules came into effect in January 1988 that established the framework and conditions for the approval of technology import contracts by the Technology Import Administration of MOFERT (later MOFTEC).[6] In order to gain government approval, the technology contract must contain certain basic provisions, including a description of the technology to be imported, the price and method of payment, risk assignment and liabilities between the parties, and duty of confidentiality. In addition, the contract must not oblige the Chinese recipient to accept "unreasonably restrictive" provisions that: limit the manner in which the Chinese recipient uses the imported technology or products made by the technology; forbid the use of imported technology after the expiration of the contract; and prevent the recipient from further developing or improving the technology, or acquiring similar or competing technology from other sources.[7] Finally the two sets of rules require the supplier of the transferred technology to warrant that it is the rightful owner of the technology, and that the technology or know-how is complete, correct, effective, and capable of accomplishing the technical targets prescribed in the contract documents.[8]

In order to obtain approval for a transaction involving the transfer of technology a feasibility study must be prepared by the Chinese party and approved by state planning authorities. After the feasibility study has been approved the technology import contract must be reviewed by the appropriate authorities.[9] In the event that a State Council department or commission reviewed the feasibility study, MOFERT/MOFTEC has the authority to review the contract. If the feasibility study was approved by authorities within a Special Economic Zone or at the provincial or municipal level, the MOFERT/MOFTEC-authorized body at such levels is responsible for reviewing the technology contract.[10] In addition to ensuring that the contract complies with the provisions of the Technology Import Regulations and Implementing Rules regarding the requisite nature of the technology to be transferred (that is, advanced and appropriate), the absence of restrictions on use, and issuance of guarantees, the approving authority will examine the contract with reference to terms of price and taxation, respective duties and liabilities of the parties, and conformity with the feasibility study.[11]

Transfers of technology to foreign investment enterprises are subject to additional provisions. The Joint Venture Law specifically allows foreign investors to contribute technology as their capital contribution in an equity joint venture, provided such technology is "genuinely advanced and appropriate to China's needs."[12] The Joint Venture Implementing Regulations require the contributed technology to be "appropriate and advanced" so as to enable the products of the equity joint venture to be competitive on the international market or display "conspicuous social and economic results" on the domestic market.[13] In addition, the Implementing Regulations require technology contributed as part of the initial foreign investment to be capable of satisfying one of the following conditions: manufacturing new products urgently needed in China or suitable for export; improving the quality of existing products and raising productivity; or saving inputs in production processes.[14] Similar requirements are imposed for the transfers of technology in connection with cooperative joint ventures and wholly foreign-owned enterprises.[15]

Under the State Council's 22 Articles on encouraging investment, investment enterprises designated as "advanced technology enterprises" are accorded a number of preferential benefits, including exemption from the payment of state subsidies for enterprise staff and workers, extension of priority status for infrastructural requirements and utilities supplies, priority in obtaining short-term loans, limits on site use fees for land located outside of busy urban sectors, and tax relief.[16] In order to qualify as an advanced technology enterprise, a foreign investment enterprise initially must satisfy the general standard set forth in Article 2(1) of the 22 Articles, which states that the enterprise provide technology and engage in developing new products or the upgrading or replacement of existing products in order to increase foreign exchange through the sale of exports or import substitution methods.[17] In addition, the foreign enterprise must demonstrate that its technology satisfies certain specified criteria: The technology production processes or critical equipment used by the enterprise must be contained on the list of technologies encouraged or desired by the central government; they must be "appropriate and advanced" in nature; and be either in short supply, able to increase exports or import substitutes, or have the potential of developing new products.[18]

Intellectual Property Legislation

Since the mid-1980s China has gradually come to recognize the close connection between providing an environment with protections for intellectual property rights and the willingness of foreign investors to engage in the transfer of technology. To encourage foreign investors to bring their advanced technological equipment, designs, and processes with them, China has promulgated legislation in the areas of patent, trademark, and copyright law.

Trademark Protection

The first area of intellectual property rights (IPR) protection in China after reform involved trademarks. In 1983 China replaced its 1963 Regulations Governing Trademarks with the Trademark Law of the People's Republic of China.[19] The Trademark Law differs from the earlier rules by establishing a new administrative structure; detailing the rights associated with a registered trademark; clarifying the actions that constitute infringement and providing additional remedies and sanctions.[20] Implementing regulations for the Trademark Law further refined the procedures for trademark protection and enforcement.[21]

Under the Trademark Law and its implementing regulations, foreign businesses seeking to obtain protection for their trademarks must retain an agent authorized by the State Administration for Industry and Commerce. The Trademark Implementing Rules have provided greater flexibility for foreign businesses in selecting an authorized agent. Although China operates under a first-to-register system, the difficulties this approach presented to foreign registrants was lessened when China became a signatory to the Paris Convention, thus permitting an applicant registered in any other Paris Convention member country to claim a six-month priority for its filings.

The application for trademark must specify the product or products to which the mark applies: Protection is limited to the product specifically listed by the applicant.[22] After an application (including a copy of the requested trademark) is submitted to the Trademark Office of the SAIC, the office conducts a preliminary examination. Upon obtaining preliminary approval the proposed trademark is published for public review and comment. If there is no justified opposition to the published trademark, a registration certificate is issued. Although there are some specific guidelines on allowable trademarks,[23] the Trademark Office has broad discretion in ruling upon trademark applications. Originally, the decision of the Trademark Review and Adjudication Board of the Trademark Office was final, although with the enactment of the Administrative Litigation Law[24] judicial review of the Board's decisions may be available.

There are certain benefits and duties that accrue to the owners of trademarks in China. Of particular significance is the requirement that the owners of trademarks bear responsibility for the quality of the goods on which the trademark is used.[25] In its role as a consumer protection agency, the Trademark Office may order unsafe or poorly manufactured goods to be remedied, otherwise the trademark holder may be faced with the imposition of fines and cancellation of his or her trademark. The trademark holders may amend their marks and license or assign their rights after obtaining the approval of the Trademark Office.

Trademark owners are protected against acts of infringement. Infringement is defined under the Trademark Law to be the use of an identical or similar mark on similar or identical goods; making or selling of representations of a registered mark on other goods; and causing prejudice to the exclusive rights of a trademark holder.[26] The Trademark Law and Implementing Rules provide for administrative sanctions against trademark violators and compensation for the economic losses incurred by the trademark owner. Both the Trademark Office and the People's Court have original jurisdiction to hear infringement matters. If proceedings are initiated at the Trademark Office, as most cases are, an appeal may be brought before the People's Court.

Patent Legislation

Prior to enacting its own patent legislation, China joined the World Intellectual Property Organization (WIPO) in March 1983 and signed the Paris Convention for the Protection of Industrial Property in December 1984.[27] The Patent Law of the People's Republic of China and its implementation regulations both came into effect on April 1, 1985.[28]

The Patent Law offers protection to inventions, utility models, and designs that possess novelty, inventiveness, or practical applicability. The Patent Implementing Regulations define an invention to be any new technical solution relating to a product or process; a utility model to be any new technical solution relating to the shape or structure of a product; and a design to be any new shape, pattern, or color of a product.[29] The terms "novelty," "inventiveness," and "practical applicability" are sometimes applied differently in China than they are in the U.S. patent law system: China adopts different standards for different types of patents whereas the United States adheres to a single standard.[30] Thus, an invention will not lose its novelty if it is publicly disclosed or used outside of China so long as the prospective patent holder files an application within six months of such disclosure.[31]

The Patent Law grants protection to foreign persons and enterprises to the extent that their home country has concluded an agreement with China or is a party to any international agreements entered into by both countries. Foreigners are defined to be those persons or enterprises that do not have a residence or business office in China. Depending upon one's status as a foreigner or Chinese entity or person, there are differing application procedures. Foreign companies registering patents as part of a technology transfer arrangement are required to provide evidence of patent registration in another country.

After receiving an application for an invention the Patent Office conducts a substantive examination at the request of the applicant. Failure to submit such a request within three years of the filing date results in the rejection of the application. For utility models or design patents, the Patent Office conducts a preliminary review and then publishes the application in the Patent Gazette. In the event there is no justified opposition, patent approval is granted. Procedures are available for internal reviews by the Patent Reexamination Board and appeals to the People's Court for review of decisions granting or refusing invention patent protection are available. However, no judicial review is available under the Patent Law for decisions on utility models or design patents.[32]

Upon approval patent protection dates back to the time of filing. Under the original Patent Law, invention patents were protected for a term of fifteen years, whereas utility models or design patents had a five-year term with a three-year renewal period. The patentee has an obligation to bring the patent into effect by using or producing the patented item, or by authorizing others to do so, within three years, otherwise the Patent Office may grant a compulsory license to exploit the patent.[33] The subject of patent protection for an invention or utility model is determined by the content of the patent claim, while for designs reference is made to the drawings and photographs.

Patent infringement is generally defined under the Patent Law as any act exploiting the patent, including manufacture, sale, or use of the patented item, without the authorization of the patent owner. There are a number of activities that do not constitute infringement such as "use without knowledge" and "use for scientific research."[34] Civil and criminal sanctions are available for parties found guilty of patent infringement.

In March 1988 the municipal governments of Beijing and Shanghai each enacted procedures providing for the resolution of patent disputes through mediation conducted by the municipal patent administration bureaus.[35] Both sets of rules were an attempt to provide additional remedies and forums for disputes involving patents beyond the relief set forth in the Patent Law and Implementing Regulations.

Copyright

Prior to 1989, China had no copyright law. Foreign transferors of copyrighted items such as technical manuals and computer software were forced to use contract provisions to protect their property. However, the limits imposed by the Technical Import Regulations and Technical Import Implementing Rules, combined with the difficulties in controlling contract performance and the behavior of noncontracting parties, made this approach generally ineffective. Among foreign investors with projects in China, the absence of a copyright law was one of the most complained-of deficiencies of the Chinese legal system prior to 1989.

B. China's Technology Transfer Regime Since 1989

Under the terms of the Agreement on Trade Relations entered into between the United States and China on July 7, 1979, both countries agreed to ensure protection of trademarks, patents, and copyrights.[36] After China failed to enact copyright legislation throughout the 1980s, the Office of the United States Trade Representative (USTR) threatened to place China on the Section 301 priority list under the 1988 Omnibus Trade and Competitiveness Act.[37] In May 1989 the USTR and MOFERT entered into a Memorandum of Understanding (MOU) by which China agreed to strengthen its legal protections for foreign enterprises in China, while the United States agreed in return not to place China on the Section 301 priority list.[38] The MOU stipulated that China would provide a draft of a copyright law to the State Council and National People's Congress by the end of 1989, provide protection for computer programs, and expand the scope and term of patent protection.

The Copyright Law of the PRC

China enacted its Copyright Law in 1990 and implementing regulations for the law the following year.[39] The Copyright Law defines a copyright as including both "economic" and "moral" rights, which are the rights to publish, revise, protect a work, and use it for monetary gain. There are limits placed on these rights thereby allowing others to use a work without providing remuneration for the purposes of: reproducing works for private use, study, research, and entertainment purposes; quoting or publishing a work for circulation in the media; and translating or copying limited quantities of a work for use in teaching or cultural and governmental activities.[40] Uses that are generally beyond the scope of these limitations require an authorization contract be entered into between the copyright owner and user.

Copyrightable works include printed, visual, and audio material, as well as diagrams, designs and computer software. Although copyrights generally belong to the creator of a work, they may attach to an employer or other legal entity if the work is created in the course of employment or completed primarily with material support from an employer. The right of a creator to publish, use, and receive compensation for a work extends for the life of the creator plus fifty years if a natural person and fifty years from the year of creation if a legal person, such as a business association. For natural or legal persons in China a copyright comes into existence upon the date of the creation of the work. For foreigners a copyright begins on the date that the works are first published in China, or for works published outside of China, within thirty days after initial foreign publication.[41] The Copyright Law does not specifically protect the works of foreigners first published outside of China, but leaves this to multilateral or bilateral agreements to which China is a party. In January 1992 a second MOU was entered into between the United States and China by which China agreed to accede to the Berne Convention on Protection of Literary and Artistic Works by October 1992.[42] The Convention permits foreign copyright owners to obtain rights of priority for copyrighted property first registered outside of China.[43]

Infringement is defined under the Copyright Law to be the publication or reproduction of another's work without permission, or using the work without providing compensation. Infringers may be required to discontinue the infringement, eliminate the creator's damages, pay compensation, or make a public apology. There are no criminal sanctions. Infringement disputes may be resolved by conciliation, arbitration, or court adjudication.

Computer Software Regulations

Although the Copyright Law included software as a protected item, it stated that software would be addressed in a separate set of rules.[44] On October 1, 1991 China promulgated the Computer Software Protection Regulations,[45] which provide protection for computer software that is either first published in China or created by the nationals of countries that have entered into bilateral agreements with China or multilateral agreements to which China is a party. Even though concerns remain over the provision for registration of software as a condition for receiving protection, the regulations were seen as a major first step toward effective protection of foreign software.

Patent and Trademark Reform

Under both the 1989 and 1992 MOUs China had agreed to amend its Patent Law to extend the scope and duration of patent protection. In January 1993 China amended its Patent Law, extending the duration of patents to twenty years for inventions and ten years for utility models and industrial designs.[46] The revised law also extended patent protection to chemical formulas, permitting patents to be issued for pharmaceuticals and agricultural chemicals, for example, and foods and beverages. The Regulations for the Administrative Protection of Pharmaceuticals expanded on the protection regime applicable to these products.[47] Finally, also as part of the 1992 MOU with the United States, the Trademark Law was amended in February 1993, effective July 1, 1993, to provide additional protections for registered trademarks.[48] The 1993 Trademark Amendments have extended the definition of infringement to include the knowing sale of counterfeit goods. The amendments also provide for criminal penalties for infringers, and trademarks that were obtained by deceptive or improper means may be canceled by the Trademark Office. Finally the 1993 Trademark Amendments extended coverage of the Trademark Law to service marks.

* * *

Perhaps more than in any other area of China's foreign economic relations, the provisions on technology transfer have revealed the effects of conflicting domestic priorities and foreign pressures. Nonetheless, the Chinese government has successfully put in place a significant array of laws and regulations to ensure that technology transfers to China are conducted with due regard to China's national interests while also giving due regard to the protection of foreign intellectual property interests.

II. Performance of China's Technology Transfer System

One measure of performance of China's technology transfer regime involves the continued prominence that technology plays in China's foreign business transactions. Technology transfers to China have continued to play a major role in China's foreign economic relations. During the 1980s, the number of transactions grew from U.S.$2 billion in 1981–84 combined to nearly U.S.$3 billion in 1989.[49] Often direct foreign investment projects involved the transfer of technology as a component of the foreign investor's capital contribution.[50] The conditions for technology transfer improved following the conclusion in 1989 of China's bilateral agreement with the United States on intellectual property protection.[51] The ever-increasing emphasis given to advanced technology enterprises in China's investment inducement efforts has also contributed to the continued importance of technology transfers in China's foreign economic relations.[52] Indeed in 1992, the Chinese government intensified the requirements for enterprises obtaining status as "advanced technology enterprises" by requiring that the technology involved be advanced by world standards, as opposed to Chinese standards as was the case with the previous regulations issued in 1988.[53]

Yet the performance of China's technology transfer system is not expressed merely in the continued expansion of technology transfer projects in China. From the perspective of foreign businesses, the performance of China's technology transfer regime involves primarily the extent to which intellectual property is effectively protected. This entails an interplay between the use of contractual protection mechanisms and the public protection system expressed through laws and patents, trademarks, and copyrights.

As indicated by the U.S. negotiating positions leading up to the 1989 Sino–U.S. memorandum of understanding on intellectual property protection, and by the position of the GATT parties concerning China's accession, foreign governments and business interests were generally dissatisfied with the performance of China's intellectual property regime during the 1980s.[54] The legal protections offered to intellectual property were seen as inadequate, while those laws that were enacted were not enforced effectively.

As a result of these perceived inadequacies, foreign technology owners were left to rely on business contracts to protect their intellectual property. However, the Technology Import Contract Regulations and their Implementing Rules sought to diminish the capacity of foreign technology licensors to limit the activities of their licensees.[55] Despite these provisions, foreign technology transferors continued to rely on contracts as the basis for protection of intellectual property. Exceptions to the regulatory restrictions were sought and often granted on the grounds that China's intellectual property protection system was inadequate and contracts were the only method of protecting the licensor's intellectual property rights. Thus, technology licensing agreements were permitted to contain standard terms prohibiting unauthorized use or duplication of the licensed technology and to impose on licensees a positive duty to take effective measures to prevent such activities. Monitoring arrangements were also included that required licensees to detect infringements and notify the licensor. Limitations on use of the technology both during and after duration of the license were common.

The formalism evident in other aspects of the legal regimes governing China's foreign economic relations has had effects in the technology transfer area as well. The enactment of laws on protection of patents, trademarks, and copyright—to a large extent as a result of U.S. pressure and the conclusion of two memoranda of understanding—have in the minds of many implementing officials removed the rationale for flexible enforcement of the technology import regulations and their implementing rules. Technology licensing agreements that impose limits on the use of the technology during and after the duration of the license are routinely rejected by the approval authorities. Contractual requirements that the licensee be responsible for monitoring and private enforcement are no longer easily available. Thus, as a result of the formalistic approach to intellectual property protection taken by Chinese regulatory officials, technology licensing transactions are increasingly dependent on enforcement of the public law regime for protecting intellectual property.

However, despite the formal completion of the main elements of the legal regime, enforcement remains a problem. As with the enactment of public laws in other sectors, legal regulation does not often result in widespread compliance. Foreign business operators continually complain about infringements.[56] Street markets and even formally licensed shops in China often display unauthorized copies of foreign literary and computer works. Despite China's accession to the WIPO treaty, foreign-registered patents and trademarks remain vulnerable to copying and foreign businesses must constantly be vigilant to detect attempts to register their patents and trademarks in alternative classifications.[57] There have been instances in which foreign-registered patents for inventions have been copied and registered as industrial designs—sometimes by Chinese business partners of foreign firms. The trademark area is even more difficult because of the requirement of registration in specifically identified classifications (for example, food and beverage trademarks registered in classifications for glassware), which permits unauthorized registration by unlicensed Chinese firms of the same trademark in other classifications (for instance, clothing or headwear).

A major component of the enforcement problem concerns the role of administrative enforcement, which devolves significant discretion to local officials. Despite provisions permitting parties claiming infringement to bring action directly to the courts, enforcement remains largely in the hands of local administrative agencies.[58] Foreign businesses that detect infringements have little choice but to rely on the efforts of local departments of the Patent, Trademark, or Copyright administrations to chase down and punish violators. Aside from the very real problems that exist where local regulators have parochial interests that discourage them from pursuing infringement cases vigorously, there remains the problem that the local enforcing agencies lack the power to prohibit and punish infringements. The sanctions permitted under the relevant intellectual property laws and regulations emphasize cease and desist orders and the role of apology in resolving infringement problems.[59] Even where a penalty is levied, enforcement requires intervention by the local Public Security Bureau (possibly, but not always with involvement by the local Procuracy or People's Court), whose parochial interests are not served by vigorous actions against local enterprises. And even when enforced, the applicable penalties are often woefully inadequate.

Thus, the critical role of local officials in administering the intellectual property system represents a significant obstacle to effective enforcement. As with other aspects of the Chinese regulatory environment, local officials have broad discretion to interpret and implement policy, and this discretion is often employed in pursuit of local interests. As a result, effective action against infringers is often delayed or prevented altogether.

III. Attitudes Affecting Performance of the System

The formalism that has permitted the regulation of technology transfers and associated intellectual property concerns to move from private contract to the realm of public law is not unique to this aspect of China's foreign economic relations. But it does have particular effects in the context of intellectual property in the way that it interacts with other attitudes. Formalistic approaches ignore the effects of traditional Chinese views about emulation and copying, while complementing socialist notions about property and the approaches taken by many developing countries concerning the role of technology in development.

In the culture and society of traditional China, copying was not viewed with disdain. Whether copying the masters in the realm of paintings or poetry or in the repetition of Confucian classics during the official examinations, emulation was seen as an exercise in deference as well as a socialization exercise.[60] Thus, there is not the basic social opprobrium attached to copying that serves as the cultural foundation for Western notions about intellectual property. This contributes to problems with enforcement of intellectual property rules since these rules are not consonant with basic underlying cultural views on the autonomy of the creative exercise.

Formalistic approaches to technology transfers are also affected by the socialist critique of private property. Despite policy changes that have permitted increasingly broad rights to private property,[61] the ideological view that property is an inherently exploitive relationship remains available if not to reduce popular reliance on private property then certainly to justify official and private intrusions on property rights. Thus, in contrast to the cultural icons that exist in the West about private property, private property in the PRC is a policy creation rather than a basic right.[62] The absence of deeply entrenched notions about the sanctity of private property is of particular relevance to intellectual property relations, where the property in question is abstract rather than tangible. Thus, the recognition of intellectual property rights represents a limited exception to the general norms of Chinese socialist ideology that restrict private property rights, and does not carry with it the requirement of strict and effective enforcement as a condition for the recognition to be meaningful.

The formalism evident in Chinese attitudes toward technology transfer also reflects approaches to the North–South conflict and the role of technology in development. Reflective of United Nations resolutions on the New International

Economic Order, Chinese policies express the view that the developed countries of the world have a duty to assist others in development.[63] Implicit in this view are conclusions of dependency theorists that the development of the technology and capital-rich countries of the "North" was made possible through the exploitation of the less-developed countries (LDCs) of the "South." The "right" of the LDCs to receive development assistance carries with it an implied right to acquire technology on the most favorable terms possible. Thus, laws and policies concerning technology transfer are seen as products of limited necessity—that of doing the minimum necessary to induce transfers of foreign technology licensing rather than to meet the broader concern of protecting basic property rights. These attitudes are reflected in the compulsory licensing provisions of the PRC Patent Law, which impose on foreign technology owners a duty to make or use the patented product or process in China.[64] In the context of the perceived inadequacies of China's intellectual property protection system, this requirement has been seen as compelling foreign technology owners to make their patents available for unauthorized pirating in China. More specific claims have been raised that the compulsory licensing requirements have been enforced discriminatorily against Western technology licensors and also have been used improperly in licensing negotiations.[65]

In light of these basic attitudes, Chinese policies and laws governing technology transfers become more clear. Against a backdrop of traditional attitudes that tend to downplay the importance of intellectual property in general, Chinese approaches reflect concern with property rights and development. The willingness to impose restrictions on technology transfer contract terms reflects basic attitudes against protecting exploitive property rights and permitting Chinese development to be held hostage by foreign business interests. These attitudes are also evident in China's reluctance to enact and then to enforce vigorously an intellectual property laws system. Once China bowed to foreign pressure in creating a public law system for protecting intellectual property rights, Chinese policy views on private property and development then required that this system replace the private contract system as the basis for intellectual property protection even if it is inadequate in the enforcement area.

The formalism of this approach, which assumes the effective operation of the intellectual property protection system on the basis of the enactment of legislation rather than on the basis of empirical reality, was evident in the Chinese "White Paper on Intellectual Property Rights," issued in June 1994.[66] The White Paper makes little effort to articulate specific proposals to improve China's intellectual property protection system, and instead criticizes calls from the United States and other countries for improvements in China's practices of IPR protection as unfounded.

IV. Implications

Although technology transfer will remain an important component in China's foreign economic relations, it will remain dependent on intellectual property protection. Even if present trends continue and foreign investment continues unabated, China's capacity to attract truly advanced and high-quality technology as a component of investment projects will require more effective measures to protect intellectual property. Moreover, if foreign investment in China stabilizes or declines, China may lose its ability to require technology transfer as the price of participation in China's economic growth, and indeed may find itself in a position of having to cajole and persuade foreign businesses to transfer technology. In such a case intellectual property protection will take on even greater importance. Although the system is still new and firm conclusions remain somewhat tentative, the evident problems with effective enforcement suggest that intellectual property remains a problem for foreign technology owners seeking to do business in China. Indeed the event precipitating the 1994 White Paper was yet another U.S. threat of a Special 301 investigation. Unless the formal contents of the system are put into effective practice, technology transfers to China will not reach their potential.

CHAPTER 5

Taxation and Foreign Exchange

I. The Legal Regime Governing Foreign Exchange and Taxation of Foreign Business in China

The regulatory regime governing the financial aspects of foreign business operations in China may usefully be examined by reference to the systems for foreign exchange and taxation. Although these are not the only aspects of finance that relate to China's foreign economic relations, they are arguably the most important because they have a direct effect on revenues and profits.

A. Foreign Exchange

Prior to 1980, China's currency was for the most part not convertible on the world market. Beginning in 1980 and lasting until the reform of the foreign exchange system effective January 1, 1994, China had a two-currency system. The domestic currency (*renminbi* or RMB) was intended for use exclusively in the local economy, whereas the convertible currency (*waihuijuan* or foreign exchange certificates) was intended for use in connection with China's foreign economic relations. The system gave the central authorities effective opportunities to control China's balance of payments. Beginning in 1994, the *waihuijuan* was abolished, and China's currency was again unified. The bulk of the following discussion will address the two-currency system, but a brief introduction to the recent reforms will be included.

The Dual Currency Foreign Exchange System

With the opening up of China's economy in the late 1970s, foreign exchange was tightly controlled by central authorities responsible for coordinating import requirements on the basis of export earnings. The establishment of the "open door policy" created a need for the convertibility of China's currency, *renminbi* (RMB). Although the government responded by issuing foreign exchange certificates (FEC) in 1980, it continued to control exchange rates and administer foreign exchange funds. This governmental control was clarified in several early pieces of legislation.

Under the Provisional Regulations on Foreign Exchange Control all foreign exchange transactions were to be made in accordance with the foreign exchange plan, prepared by the State Administration of Exchange and Control (SAEC), approved by the State Council, and supervised by the Bank of China (BOC) and MOFERT (later MOFTEC).[1] Joint ventures were required to comply with the Foreign Exchange Law and encouraged to export their products in order to earn foreign exchange.[2] Although profits could be repatriated, in principle each venture was to balance its foreign exchange account held by the BOC. The enactment of the Foreign Exchange Control Implementing Rules and Joint Venture Implementing Rules in 1983 provided additional detail on foreign exchange control requirements.[3] Both sets of rules continued to emphasize the need to balance foreign exchange, but provided some means for preventing and resolving imbalances.

The Joint Venture Law Implementing Rules set forth the procedures by which joint ventures were to control and account for their foreign exchange through the offices of the Bank of China. Joint ventures were urged to obtain their inputs from the domestic market and sell their products on international markets. In clarifying the domestic sale option put forward in the 1979 Joint Venture Law, the Implementing Regulations explained that the products of a joint venture that a Chinese foreign trade company needed to import could be sold to such a company for foreign currency.[4] These rules also permitted joint ventures to obtain foreign currency loans from the Bank of China or overseas banking institutions. In the event that a foreign exchange imbalance persisted, the imbalance could be resolved by accessing the foreign exchange reserves of the relevant government department in charge of the joint venture project or through the inclusion of the joint venture project in the economic plan after review and approval by MOFERT and the State Planning Commission.[5]

The Foreign Exchange Control Implementing Rules provided additional details on foreign exchange monitoring. Budgets of proposed foreign exchange transactions and statements of actual transactions were to be submitted annually, while quarterly reports were to be submitted to the SAEC for any overseas foreign exchange accounts. All foreign exchange transactions were to be at the rate prescribed by the SAEC. The Foreign Exchange Implementing Rules also detailed the numerous procedures joint ventures must follow to gain access to their foreign currency reserves on deposit in their bank accounts to remit profits. This included the submission of applications and numerous documents to the appropriate bank branch and the SAEC.

For many joint ventures this regulatory framework created problems, which were exacerbated by the foreign exchange crises China faced in 1984 and 1985.[6] In response to the difficulties foreign investors faced in balancing their foreign exchange, the State Council issued new rules in January 1986 to resolve these problems.[7] Although the 1986 Forex Balancing Regulations reiterated the need for foreign investors to export their products and balance their foreign exchange expenditures and receipts, they also provided some substantive measures by which joint ventures could generate or obtain additional foreign exchange provided they met their export obligations. The Forex Balancing Regulations lessened the obstacles for import substitution sales in China by requiring the appropriate governmental authorities to assist in arranging for Chinese enterprises to enter into import substitution arrangements. The steps by which a foreign partner in a joint venture could reinvest its RMB profits in a Chinese export-oriented enterprise were also clarified. Several new approaches for supplementing the foreign exchange earnings of joint ventures were introduced in the Forex Balancing Regulations. These included the purchase in RMB of domestic products by a foreign investment enterprise for sale on international markets, and the adjustment of a joint venture's foreign exchange deficit with a joint venture having a foreign exchange surplus and a common parent in a holding-company-type relationship. This requirement excluded many joint ventures, of course, because they were not part of a larger holding company structure.

The State Council's 22 Articles on encouraging foreign investment extended the concept of adjusting foreign exchange surpluses and deficits by allowing all foreign investment enterprises, regardless of their equity or corporate structure, to engage in adjustments with each other.[8] Additionally the 22 Articles introduced a procedure by which foreign investment enterprises with foreign exchange surpluses could deposit them in a bank within China as collateral for a loan in the equivalent amount of RMB. Although this tended to tie up the foreign exchange holdings of the enterprise, it allowed the enterprise to regain its foreign exchange upon repayment of the loan in RMB, rather than forego title to its foreign currency as required under the Joint Venture Implementing Rules.

Implementing regulations issued pursuant to the 22 Articles introduced additional measures to assist foreign investment enterprises further with their foreign exchange problems. For example, MOFERT issued measures detailing the procedures for the purchase and export of domestically produced goods by foreign investment enterprises.[9] These were generally well received, although companies seeking to avail themselves of these provisions often found themselves competing with local enterprises in the sourcing of products for export.

In 1989 the SAEC introduced regulations elaborating on earlier import substitution provisions that permitted the domestic sale for foreign exchange of goods produced by foreign investment enterprises, provided the goods are among those that would have to be imported by Chinese enterprises.[10] And unlike the earlier import substitution rules issued by the State Planning Commission in late 1987, the new SAEC measures did not require joint ventures to obtain import substitution status prior to the time they were established.[11] Furthermore, the list of eligible goods was expanded beyond earlier limited lists of "technologically advanced products" or products needed by central or local governments in the short term, to include goods needed under the state plan or to be imported through the payment of foreign exchange by domestic enterprises.[12]

One of the most significant developments in the later half of the 1980s was the expansion of the currency swap system initiated under the 22 Articles.[13] Starting in 1985 in Shenzhen, swap markets, formally known as Foreign Exchange Adjustment Centers (FEACs), were established whereby FIEs could trade RMB and foreign exchange. Although no national legislation has been promulgated on swap centers specifically, many provincial and municipal governments throughout China allowed and encouraged the operation of FEACs. By 1992 there were over ninety FEACs throughout China operating under the guidance of local branches of the SAEC.[14] Although the operating rules for FEACs differed from one city or province to the next, the rate at which foreign exchange was traded was generally higher than the official rate, but lower than the black market rate.

Currency Unification and Foreign Exchange Reform

In December 1993, and effective January 1, 1994, the "Foreign Exchange Certificates" were formally abolished.[15] However, the RMB was not yet made freely convertible. Under the reforms, foreign currencies will be exchanged through various authorized banks and will still be subject to administrative controls. Initially there were thirteen such banks, including those in the state bank system as well as specialized banks such as the Bank of Communications and the Industrial Bank of the China International Trust and Investment Corporation (CITIC). An interbank market is expected to be established to set the exchange rate. In April 1994, new regulations were issued on the settlement and sales of foreign exchange.[16] These measures provide for the establishment of foreign exchange accounts at Chinese banks by Chinese and foreign-funded enterprises and require enterprises to sell their foreign exchange earnings to one or more authorized banks.

For the moment the FIEs are not overly involved in the new system. FIEs were exempted from the mandatory sales provision in the settlement regulations, and are permitted to retain their foreign exchange earnings to pay debt service and other expenses. The FIEs are expected to continue relying on the swap centers to exchange their RMB earnings for foreign currency. Nonetheless, the reforms are an indicator of further changes to come as China's currency becomes completely freely convertible. The reform measures contemplate the gradual elimination of the swap markets, as foreign businesses deal directly with banks to exchange their RMB earnings for foreign currency.

The reform of China's foreign exchange system will likely reduce the cost to foreign businesses of balancing their Chinese and foreign currency income and expenses. At the same time, it may well increase foreign businesses' access to the Chinese domestic market, as Chinese enterprises become freer to enter transactions with foreign businesses based on market considerations rather than the bureaucratic concerns of foreign exchange balancing. In concert with contemplated changes in China's state banking system,[17] the foreign exchange reforms are likely to have broad repercussions for foreign business in China. However, many substantive and procedural details must be finalized before a clear picture will emerge of the operational reality of China's foreign exchange reform.

B. Taxation

The enactment in 1991 of a unified taxation scheme that combined under one statute the arrangements pertaining to foreign investment enterprises and foreign enterprises represented a major reform in the PRC's foreign tax system. The reformed system still bears the effects of the pre-1991 regime, however, and should be examined by reference to previous tax schemes.

Foreign Investment and Foreign Enterprise Taxation Prior to July 1991

Prior to 1991, the Chinese foreign taxation system was centered on separate treatment for foreign enterprises and foreign investment enterprises.[18] This reflected the extent to which joint ventures were seen initially as a limited experiment that should be viewed and treated separately from the rest of China's foreign economic ties. This approach evolved as Chinese policy and the resulting character and structure of China's foreign business ties changed.

Joint Venture Income Tax Law

Originally, income of joint ventures was taxed under the Joint Venture (JV) Income Tax Law enacted in September 1979; its implementing regulations were enacted the following year.[19] Under these measures, all worldwide income of an equity joint venture derived from "production and business operations" and "other income" was taxable. Income was defined to be net income after the deduction of costs, expenses, and losses, and was taxed at a flat tax rate of 30 percent plus a local surtax of 10 percent of the tax. In addition a 10 percent withholding tax was imposed on profits remitted outside of China by a foreign equity participant. There were several means for obtaining tax reductions or exemptions based on incentives set forth in the Joint Venture Income Tax Law. These included an exemption for the first two profit-making years of the equity joint venture and a 50 percent reduction in the following three years. Furthermore foreign participants reinvesting their profits in their or another joint venture were eligible for refunds of up to 40 percent of the income tax paid on the reinvested funds.

Foreign Enterprise Income Tax Law

Prior to 1982 there were no laws regarding taxation on the income of foreign enterprises, other than equity joint ventures. The Foreign Enterprise Income Tax Law and its accompanying Implementing Rules, both enacted in 1982, established a separate tax regime for foreign companies, enterprises, or other economic organizations operating in China other than through joint ventures.[20] Under these measures, foreign enterprises having an "establishment" in China were taxed at rates varying from 20-40 percent plus a 10 percent local surcharge,[21] whereas foreign businesses without "establishments" were taxed on a withholding basis at a flat 20 percent rate. An establishment was defined as an organization, site, or business agent in China engaging in production or business operations: Foreign representative offices were included within the definition of an establishment. Fewer exemptions and reductions were available under the Enterprise Tax Law as compared to the Joint Venture Tax Law.[22]

Preferential Tax Policies of the SEZ, ETDZs, and Coastal Cities

Foreign enterprises and joint ventures with investments in the Special Economic Zones (SEZs), Economic and Technological Development Zones (ETDZs), and open Coastal Cities were granted special tax benefits. Under tax reduction measures enacted in 1984, all foreign investment enterprises located in the SEZs and open Coastal Cities were subject to a flat 15 percent income tax.[23] The 1984 SEZ/ETDZ Tax Reduction Regulations also extended the five-year tax holidays available to equity joint ventures under the JV Tax Law to all foreign investment enterprises that operated in the production sector for more than ten years. Foreign enterprises in the service sector were eligible for three-year tax holidays. In addition, under the 1984 SEZ/ETDZ Tax Reduction Regulations, withholding taxes were reduced or waived, and exemptions and reductions from payments due under Industrial and Commercial Consolidated Tax (ICCT) were available. The SEZs and ETDZs also had specific preferential tax packages thereby further reducing the tax liability of foreign investors or businesses.[24]

The 1986 Provisions for the Encouragement of Foreign Investment

The State Council's 22 Articles investment inducement package offered additional tax reductions. Foreign investment enterprises that satisfied the conditions for designation as a "technologically advanced enterprise" could prolong their initial three-year tax holiday for an additional three years. Joint ventures meeting the "export enterprise" criteria were eligible for a 50 percent reduction in the amount of tax due during any year that their exports exceeded 70 percent of their total production value. Foreign participants in technologically advanced enterprises and export enterprises were exempt from the withholding tax on profits remitted outside of China and could obtain a total refund for income tax already paid on reinvested profits, provided those profits were reinvested in China for a period of at least five years.

The Unified Tax Regime

The bifurcated system of taxation that treated equity joint venture differently from cooperative enterprises and wholly foreign-owned enterprises was increasingly problematic. Foreign investors faced significant tax consequences deriving from choices as to the form rather than the content and operation of their business enterprises in China: The tax bill under a 33 percent effective rate for equity joint ventures could be significantly lower than that applicable to cooperative enterprises and wholly foreign-owned enterprises under the progressive rate system of the Foreign Enterprise Tax Law.

In response to these problems, China unified the tax law applicable to foreign business in 1991 with the enactment of the Income Tax Law of the People's Republic of China for Enterprises with Foreign Investment and Foreign Enterprises (hereafter "Unified Foreign Enterprise Tax Law" or UFETL).[25] The UFETL includes equity joint ventures, cooperative enterprises, and wholly foreign-owned enterprises under the rubric of "foreign investment enterprises," while leaving other foreign business activities such as representative offices under the category of "foreign enterprises." The taxable income of FIEs and foreign enterprises with establishments or sites in China is subject to a basic effective tax rate of 33 percent, whereas the income of foreign enterprises without establishments in China is taxed on a withholding basis at a 20 percent rate.

The UFETL incorporates many of the preferential tax provisions applicable under previous law for enterprises in the SEZs, ETDZs, and open Coastal Cities.[26] Thus, FIEs and foreign enterprises engaged in business or production operations in a SEZ or ETDZ are provided with a base income tax rate of 15 percent. Production-oriented FIEs established in open Coastal Cities or in the old urban districts of SEZs or ETDZs are provided with a base income tax rate of 24 percent. The new tax law also reiterates the tax holidays established under the 1984 SEZ/ETDZ Tax Reduction Regulations. FIEs that are "production oriented" with operating terms in excess of ten years are exempted from paying tax for the first two years and pay a reduced rate of 50 percent of the tax due in the third through fifth years beginning with the first profit-making tax year. Additional exemptions of 15 percent to 30 percent of the tax due are available for a period of ten years for enterprises established in underdeveloped areas.

The UFETL and its Implementing Rules incorporate both the broad policies of encouraging foreign investment in technologically advanced and export-oriented industries, and the specific preferential tax policies that were established in the 22 Articles. Enterprises that export more than 70 percent of their total value output may apply for a 50 percent reduction in the amount of income tax payable in any year after their initial tax holiday and exemption period.[27] Technologically advanced enterprises may extend their 50 percent income tax reduction for three years.[28] Such extensions and reductions are dependent upon the approval of local tax authorities, and may not result in a reduction of more than 90 percent of the income tax actually due.

Although most of the provisions in the UFETL originated in earlier legislation there are some innovative aspects. One of the more notable new rules is a provision addressing the use of transfer pricing between an enterprise and its affiliates to decrease tax liabilities. Enterprises are required to deal with their affiliates in an arms-length manner or face the imposition of price readjustments by the taxing authorities.[29] The UFETL also provides new penalties for taxpayers who fail to comply with the requirements of the law, including fines and prison terms. For taxpayers who disagree with the decisions of the tax authorities, the UFETL provides more detail on the procedures for seeking a reconsideration of administrative decisions as well as for obtaining judicial review.[30]

Other Taxes

The Chinese tax regime for foreign business extends to a number of other areas. The Individual Income Tax (IIT) formed the basis for personal taxation of foreign individuals. Prior to January 1994, when it was replaced by a network of new taxes, the Industrial and Commercial Consolidated Tax (ICCT) was the primary tax levied on business turnover in China.

Individual Income Tax

The Individual Income Tax Law of the People's Republic of China (hereafter IITL) was enacted in September 1980 and Implementing Rules came into effect several months later.[31] The original IITL was amended in 1993, although this had little impact on the law's application to foreigners.[32]

In determining the amount of tax an individual may be subject to under the IITL, it is necessary first to ascertain whether the taxpayer has either a domicile or residency in China. Generally as the duration of residency increases, or if the foreign taxpayer is domiciled in China, the potential sources of income subject to Chinese taxation expand. Thus, an individual residing in China for a period of ninety days is generally required to pay tax only on income derived from China, whereas an individual residing in China in excess of five years must pay tax on all worldwide income. The IITL details the forms of income that are taxable, and the different tax rates that each form is subject to.[33] Salaries and wages are taxed progressively at rates ranging from 5 to 45 percent, whereas nonwage income is generally taxed at a 20 percent flat rate. A number of deductions are permitted thereby resulting in varying tax liabilities depending upon individual circumstances.

Although each individual income earner is responsible for paying the proper amount of tax and registering with taxing authorities, the employer generally acts as the withholding agent and must also report to taxing authorities. The tax authorities have broad investigatory powers. Individuals and their employers are subject to fines for omissions or errors in reporting and paying taxes. Taxpayers who seek to challenge the decisions of taxing authorities may pursue administrative remedies or judicial review.

Industrial and Commercial Consolidated Tax

Prior to January 1, 1994, China's primary domestic business tax was the Industrial and Commercial Consolidated Tax (ICCT).[34] The ICCT was a broad-based turnover tax imposed at various levels of economic activity as taxable goods or services are transferred from one entity to another through the production cycle as well as at the wholesale and retail level. Unlike the 1984 value-added tax, which often operated in tandem with it,[35] the ICCT did not provide any credit for taxes paid upon earlier transfers. ICCT was imposed on the production of industrial goods, the purchase of agricultural products, the importation of foreign goods, commercial retailing, and the sale of services, including communications and transportation. As the ICCT was a component of the price of a good or service it was to be remitted to the local branch of the PBOC after payment was received from the purchaser. Tax rates were set forth in the ICCT Rate Schedule and ranged from 1.5 percent to 69 percent. Depending on the category of good or service involved, lower rates or exemptions were available.

Despite its origins as a domestic tax, the ICCT was extended first to joint ventures and cooperative enterprises,[36] as well as to representative offices and wholly foreign-owned enterprises.[37] Ultimately, investment incentive measures significantly reduced the application of ICCT.[38]

The New Regime: Value Added Tax, Consumption Tax and Business Tax

Effective January 1, 1994, the ICCT was abolished, and replaced by a series of new taxes including a new Value-Added Tax (VAT), Consumption Tax, and Business Tax.[39] The Value-Added Tax applies to a wide range of goods and services.[40] The tax rates are either 13 percent (for selling or importing goods such as cereals and edible vegetable oils, tap water, reading materials, and agricultural needs such as fertilizer and pesticides) or 17 percent for all other goods and for repair or processing labor services. Exports are not subject to the VAT. The Consumption Tax applies to the production, processing, or importation of consumer goods.[41] Tax rates range from 3 percent for small automobiles to 45 percent for cigarettes, with the rate imposed against the sales value of the goods. The Business Tax applies to the provision of labor services and the transfer of tangible or intangible assets.[42] Tax rates range generally from 3 to 5 percent (except for a 20 percent tax on karaoke halls, music tea houses, billiard halls, golf, and bowling), imposed against the transfer value of the asset of service. A further Land Value-Added Tax was also enacted to impose taxes at 30 to 60 percent on the value of real estate transactions.[43] In replacing the ICCT, the new regime of transfer taxes makes clear distinctions between goods and services, and between transfers where value is added and where it is not. Although it will take time for the new system to be fully operational and subject to precise evaluation,[44] it appears initially as an attempt to bring greater precision to the turnover taxation of goods and services.

Tax Enforcement

Tax enforcement issues are generally governed by the "Law of the PRC to Administer the Levying and Collection of Taxes" and its Implementing Regulations.[45] These measures replace earlier regulations on tax administration which, while not covering individual taxation directly, offered useful insights to the regulatory thinking of the tax authorities.[46] The Tax Administration Law grants

Chinese tax authorities broad discretionary authority to conduct investigations regarding tax compliance and impose sanctions in events of noncompliance with the tax laws and regulations.[47] As a result, tax enforcement tends to involve protracted negotiations over the amount and sourcing of income and the details of payment and enforcement. Penalties for failure to comply with tax regulations range from specific fines of 2,000–10,000 yuan or more, fines in the amount of up to five times the tax deficiency, confiscation of illegal earnings, and more serious criminal and administrative penalties.[48]

In instances in which the taxpayer or withholding agent wishes to contest a finding by the tax authorities regarding payment of tax, the tax assessed must first be paid and then an application for reconsideration must be made to the next highest level of the tax bureaucracy within sixty days of receipt of the tax payment certificate.[49] These higher authorities must render a decision on the request for reconsideration within sixty days of receiving the application.[50] If unsatisfied with the review decision, the applicant must initiate legal proceedings with the People's Court within fifteen days of the date of receipt of the review decision.[51] In cases where the party concerned contests a penalty decision or other enforcement measures, application for reconsideration must be made within fifteen days of receipt of the penalty or enforcement notice.[52] Application for judicial review may be made either directly within fifteen days of receipt of the penalty or enforcement notice, or within fifteen days of receipt of the reconsideration decision.[53]

The procedures for the reconsideration process within the tax bureaucracy are set forth in the "PRC Regulations on Administrative Reconsideration," which provide general rules for administrative reconsideration decisions throughout the Chinese bureaucracy.[54] Specific rules were enacted governing reconsideration procedures in tax cases, although to the extent these conflict with the Tax Administration Law and its Implementing Regulations, those parts in conflict will not remain in effect.[55] If the taxpayer wishes to contest a reconsideration decision, an appeal may be filed with the People's Court pursuant to the Administrative Litigation Law of the PRC.

Tax Treaties

China's income tax laws, including the UFETL and the IITL, provide that the terms of tax treaties shall prevail over specific statutory provisions. By late 1987 China had entered into tax treaties with most of its major trading partners, thereby providing a more attractive environment for investors.[56] These treaties generally follow one of several models, including the OECD Model Double Taxation Convention and the United Nations Model Convention, although the

U.S.–PRC Tax Treaty tends to follow a model specifically designed by the U.S. Treasury Department.[57]

The Treaty defines "permanent establishment" to be a fixed place of business through which the business of an enterprise is wholly or partly carried on, as well as a building site, construction project, natural resource exploration, or exploitation equipment in use for more than three months, and the furnishing of services by an enterprise through employees or agents for more than half the tax year. The U.S.–PRC Tax Treaty covers all U.S. federal income taxes.

II. Performance of the Finance System

The behavior of the regulatory system pertaining to foreign exchange and taxation reflects tensions over the purposes of these regimes as being between protection of perceived Chinese short-term financial interests and being responsive to the expressed concerns of foreign business. These factors often undermine the effectiveness of the Chinese regulatory framework.

A. Foreign Exchange

China's foreign exchange system developed as a result of concerns that foreign investors and visitors not interfere unduly with the tightly controlled state-planned economy and its deliberately low-valued currency, the *renminbi* (RMB).[58] Assumptions were made that the extent of foreign involvement in the Chinese domestic economy would be limited, and hence the introduction of foreign exchange certificates (FECs) would have little domestic effect. The FEC was seen primarily as a mechanism for temporarily isolating foreign expenditures from the domestic economy. It represented the idea that the foreigner (investor or tourist) had in effect deposited with the Chinese government a certain amount of foreign currency, which would be returned when the foreigner's capital (in the case of foreign investment repatriation of dividends) or cash (in the case of tourists) departed from China. The government's tight control over imports was seen as sufficient to prevent local demand for FEC used to buy foreign-made goods. Foreign investments were seen as geared primarily toward exports, and thus their revenues would be in foreign currencies and their limited needs for RMB for local expenses could be easily managed. Thus, the FEC was introduced as a temporary measure to ease the transition from the isolationism of the Maoist economy to the interdependence of the post-Mao reform economy.

The principle of isolation as between the FEC and RMB was aimed at protecting China's short-term financial interests by protecting the national currency (RMB) from devaluation in the face of the international market and by controlling the introduction of foreign currencies into China. Soon these purposes were outstripped by events. The easing of import controls created local demand for FEC to use in buying foreign products, and what had begun as a uniform exchange rate between RMB and FEC quickly gave way to the disparate exchange rates that have characterized much of the post-Mao era.[59] These disparate exchange rates created additional financial opportunities for the Chinese treasury, however, as foreign investors and individuals were directed to continue to use FEC in their transactions at rates of exchange that made these transactions significantly more expensive than they would be if RMB were used. This in turn created disincentives to reform the system as China's treasury captured the rents generated by disparities in valuation between FEC and RMB and the resulting increased operating costs for foreign business.

Although the dual currency system had been very successful in easing the domestic economic effects of China's entry into the world economy, it has created problems for foreign business. Depending on the disparity in exchange rates as between the FEC and RMB, FEC expenditures can impose significant additional costs on foreign businesses. Foreign representative offices, for example, are not permitted to do business in RMB and so in theory they must use FEC for all local expenditures.[60] When, as was the case in late 1988, for example, the exchange rate differential between FEC and RMB is about 2:1, this requirement effectively doubles the cost of the representative office's expenses. On the other hand, foreign investment enterprises often have disparities between their RMB income from local sales and their FEC expenses from overseas purchases or dividend payments. In these circumstances, conversion of RMB to FEC at the official 1:1 exchange rate effectively reduces by half the value of the investor's local earnings.

Attempts to remedy this problem reflected the tensions between pursuit of the short-term financial benefits derived from continuing the status quo and the need to respond to foreign business concerns over the costs of the Forex system. Although the State Council's 22 Articles attempted to address this problem and laid the groundwork for the so-called swap centers as a mechanism for foreign investment enterprises in China to adjust their currency imbalances,[61] problems remained. The exchange rates permitted at the swap centers remained below the actual market rate (referred to as the "black market rate"), and thus participants at the centers still could not get full value for their currencies. Moreover, foreign representative offices were not permitted to participate because they were not considered foreign investment enterprises. Finally, the government frequently intervened to limit trading on the swap center markets in order to protect the RMB's value. In attempting to satisfy China's perceived finance interests, each of these measures added additional foreign exchange costs to foreign business operations in China.

Prior to the currency reform measures that came into effect in 1994, China's foreign exchange control system represented a major area of concern to foreign business in China. The short-term financial interest in the benefits to China of the dual currency system outweighed the willingness to respond fully to the concerns of foreign businesses and governments over the inequities and distortions that the system permitted. These problems have not necessarily vanished, as significant bureaucratic involvement in the process of converting Chinese currency into foreign currency represents continuing opportunities for government intrusion. In addition, provisions requiring Chinese enterprises to sell their foreign currency to the authorized conversion banks permit (as indeed they are intended) the state banking sector to control expenditures of foreign currency by Chinese enterprises. The potential for bureaucratic intrusion into the foreign currency and particularly renminbi finances of foreign enterprises remains significant as well. Thus, even though the foreign exchange reforms are a much-needed and laudable step, in order to be truly effective they will need to be accompanied by parallel efforts to ensure rational market-driven management of the foreign currency conversion process.

B. Taxation

The pattern of Chinese regulation of taxation reflected conflicting concerns with encouraging foreign business investment and protecting the state's financial interests. Thus, official explanations of the purpose of China's tax system for foreign business established as a prerequisite the protection of China's national interests.[62] Subject to this premise, however, the main focus has been in providing tax incentives for foreign investment under the rubric, "light tax burden, broad preferences, and ease of procedures."[63]

Tax rules were also used to encourage specific behavior on the part of foreign investors. With a general view toward using the tax system to induce foreign investment, the Joint Venture Income Tax Law (JVITL) provided specific incentives reducing and in some instances eliminating tax of JV income.[64] Regulations were issued reducing ICCT and withholding taxes for enterprises located in the Special Economic Zones and 14 Coastal Cities.[65] The SEZs and Coastal Cities themselves introduced measures to reduce further the tax burdens of foreign firms.[66] Measures to reduce individual income tax burdens on foreign firms were also introduced.[67] In what was at the time a sweeping set of concessions, the State Council's 22 Articles provided a number of tax reduction measures targeted specifically at so-called advanced technology enterprises and export-oriented enterprises.[68] Most recently, the government moved to unify the foreign tax system and eliminate the artificial and in many respects ir-rational disparities in the tax treatment of equity and cooperative joint ventures. This was explained largely as an effort to make the tax system yet more attrac-tive to foreign business.[69]

However, the Chinese foreign business tax system was also concerned with revenue raising. While China held itself out to the world by emphasizing the use of tax preferences to encourage the introduction of foreign capital and tech-nology, there was debate internally over the extent to which the taxation system should also concentrate on generating short-term tax revenues for the state.[70] Of all the early taxes, the Individual Income Tax was perhaps most explicitly directed at generating revenues from foreign staff businesses.[71] Even the much-vaunted 22 Articles did not extend tax preferences universally: Foreign repre-sentative offices were largely excluded, thus depriving a major component of foreign business activities in China of the tax benefits offered to foreign inves-tors.[72] Moreover, under the 22 Articles foreign firms were compelled to meet specific criteria for classification as either "advanced technology" or "export-oriented" firms in order to avail themselves of most of the tax reductions.[73] Despite the issuance of regulations on this classification, the process and stand-ards for achieving these classifications remained murky—as indicated by the increasingly strict requirements for classification as an "advanced technology enterprise."[74] Many suspected that the continued lack of transparency in the confirmation of status was due to concerns over controlling the distribution of tax incentives. This concern was clearly in evidence in the issuance by central finance authorities of restrictive regulations aimed at protecting the central treasury from the effects of uncoordinated local tax concessions.[75] The Chinese government's concerns with taxation as a revenue-raising measure were central to the recent regulations on administration of taxation, which state, as one of their explicit purposes, the need to protect state tax revenues.[76]

More serious in the view of many foreign firms has been the extent of infor-mal taxation of foreign business activities that seems intended to offset the investment preferences offered under the formal tax system. The operations of foreign enterprises have been levied with extensive indirect taxes in the form of exorbitant fees for services such as telecommunications and transportation, as well as taxes on land, vehicles, services, and other matters that tend to offset the beneficial effects of the tax reductions offered under the income tax system. Artificially inflated wages for workers paid to the workers' Chinese unit, which then generally does not remit the full amount to the workers themselves, as well as compulsory contributions to various employee welfare funds also repre-sent informal taxation. Ever-increasing registration and administration fees, as well as the passing through to JV by their Chinese suppliers of the burdens of the Industrial Commercial Consolidated Tax (ICCT), value-added tax,[77] and industrial products tax added to the tax burden on foreign investment, and underscored the impression that Chinese policymakers were primarily concerned with using taxation for revenue generation, albeit in disguised ways. Moreover, these alternate taxes are not covered by China's network of tax treaties and so are not creditable against the income taxes paid by foreign businesses in their home jurisdictions.[78]

The tension between the PRC tax system's attention to investment inducements and revenue generation leaves foreign business operators uncertain as to the likely performance of the system. The conflicts between the formal tax system and its informal counterparts make it difficult for foreign businesses to predict costs or forecast the tax effects of their operations. This tends to undermine the goodwill generated by tax reduction efforts.

III. Attitudes About the Use of Law in Regulating Foreign Exchange and Foreign Taxation

The tensions evident in the Chinese foreign exchange and foreign tax systems reflect the continued influences of formalism and instrumentalism. In a legal culture where laws and regulations are seen primarily as mechanisms for achieving policy results, it is not surprising that the foreign exchange and foreign taxation systems have revealed tensions over policy objectives.

For example, the creation of the swap centers as an approved mechanism for foreign exchange balancing expressed directly a willingness to rely on market forces (albeit subject to some controls) to resolve foreign exchange balancing problems in foreign investment enterprises. However, the exclusion of foreign representative offices reflected not only formalistic (and mercantilist) presumptions about the distinction between these offices' sales activities and the investment activities of FIEs, but also ignored the possibility that representative offices of companies that also have investment enterprises in China may well be able to participate indirectly in the centers while other representative offices may not enjoy such access. More important, the artificial controls over swap center rates virtually ensured the emergence of alternative markets and the possibility of arbitrage by firms willing to participate in the black market and the swap centers simultaneously. By approving the swap center markets, the government gave vent to market-oriented assumptions that in striving to balance their foreign exchange foreign firms would opt for the lawful alternative of the swap centers even if they are slightly more expensive than illegal currency trading on the black markets. Yet by tolerating the continued existence of the black markets, the regime permitted the quasi-market operations to be undermined and seemed to confirm widespread (although as yet unproven) suspicions of foreign business managers that the arbitragers are mostly made up of Chinese firms with various levels of political protection.

In the tax area, recent regulations on tax accounting represent on one hand a welcome and long-requested response to concerns expressed by many foreign businesses in China over the indeterminacy of tax calculations.[79] On the other hand, however, the regulations have been geared primarily toward the well-publicized campaign to attack tax evasion by foreign investors.[80] Aside from the questions about scapegoating, especially in an environment where tax evasion by domestic enterprises is widespread, the campaign origins of the regulation call into question its long-term use as a basis for tax accounting. Thus, the pursuit of justified and valuable long-term goals is undermined for short-term political expediency, as instrumentalist approaches to law and regulation take precedence over establishing a stable and durable regulatory framework.

Formalism, too, is evident in the use of law and regulation to achieve policy ends. The foreign tax system has often proceeded from assumptions about the effects of taxation on behavior. Tax incentives continue to serve as the mainstay of Chinese efforts to induce foreign behavior despite the widespread and well-known views of the foreign business community in China that stability and transparency are more important than short-term tax inducements. Although slightly more attention has been paid to market-based behavior in the foreign exchange area, formalistic approaches are evident here as well.

* * *

There is little debate over the extent to which the Chinese government has succeeded in enacting a wide range of regulatory measures governing the financial aspects of foreign business in China. The government has also taken active steps to try to address foreign business concerns in the areas of foreign exchange and taxation, which have led to significant improvements in the business climate. Yet the system remains troubled in the areas of performance and attitudinal foundations, which tend to distract attention from the real gains that have been made.

IV. Implications

There can be no doubt that the regulatory framework for China's foreign tax and foreign exchange regimes has become more complex and sophisticated. There is also strong evidence that the Chinese government has attempted to respond to the expressed concerns of foreign business, while also attempting to protect its own financial interests. Yet the interplay of instrumentalism and formalism in the regulatory framework may still undermine the capacity of law and regulation to offer a stable and durable basis for behavior. Instrumentalist sentiments ensure that laws and regulations remain subject to policy swings. Formalistic assumptions about the effects of law and regulation on behavior not only reinforce policy-oriented instrumentalism but also tend to ignore the role of market-based behavior. As long as the foreign tax and foreign exchange systems remain dominated by instrumentalist and formalistic thinking, they are unlikely to fully satisfy China's market needs. Moreover, they also are unlikely to meet the needs of foreign businesses that are used to operating in a market-oriented regulatory environment.

CHAPTER 6

Dispute Resolution

I. The Legal Regime For Dispute Resolution Involving Foreign Business in China

Increased levels of foreign trade and investment in China inevitably have generated a commensurate number of disputes between foreign businesses and their counterparts in China. There are several procedures available for the settlement of disputes involving foreign business interests. The Foreign Economic Contract Law (FECL) lists these as consultation, mediation, arbitration, and litigation. In keeping with practices, the FECL emphasizes that parties should seek to resolve their disputes through consultation or third-party mediation.[1] Although the FECL does not require parties to engage in consultation or mediation before seeking a remedy through arbitration or judicial proceedings, it does restrict access to the courts by disallowing parties to litigate if they have an arbitration provision in their contract or a separate arbitration agreement. On the other hand, courts and arbitral bodies routinely engage in conciliation during the course of litigation and arbitration proceedings, suggesting that despite institutional differences conciliation, arbitration, and litigation operate along a continuum of dispute resolution methods.

An important issue in the resolution of disputes concerns the determination of whether the laws of China or the home country of the foreign business person or entity that is party to the dispute are to be applied by the arbitration or judicial body.[2] With exceptions for foreign investment and natural resource projects, the FECL generally allows contracting parties to determine the law to be applied in the settlement of disputes.[3] In the event that parties have not designated the applicable law, the FECL requires the law of the country with the closest relation to the contract to be applied. In the event that China's laws are found to be deficient or lacking, the FECL directs that the laws and custom of international practice be applied to the extent that they do not harm or violate the social or public interests of China. This approach of the FECL with respect to choice of law is comparable to that of other nations. The important

70

exception in the FECL's choice of law rules concerns foreign investment enter-prises and natural resource exploitation ventures, in which the laws of China must be applied in disputes.

A. The Arbitration of Foreign Economic Disputes

China has separate arbitration systems for domestic economic contracts,[4] mari-time issues,[5] and foreign economic and trade matters. Prior to 1980, arbitration and conciliation between Chinese and foreign parties in economic and trade matters came under the jurisdiction of the Foreign Trade Arbitration Commis-sion, which was formed in 1954 under the China Council for the Promotion of International Trade (hereafter CCPIT). On February 26, 1980 the State Council converted the Foreign Trade Arbitration Commission into the Foreign Economic and Trade Arbitration Commission (hereafter FETAC). FETAC was endowed with greater responsibilities than its predecessor was as its mission was expanded to deal with disputes arising from various new forms of economic cooperation resulting from China's open policy, such as disputes in-volving foreign investment enterprises and investment transactions in the form of credit and loans extended by overseas financial institutions.[6] Arbitral bodies also have been organized under various CCPIT subcouncils located in Shan-ghai, Shenzhen, and elsewhere.

In attempting to settle disputes FETAC encouraged parties to engage first in consultations and then in conciliation. In the event these approaches were un-successful, the dispute could be submitted to arbitration.[7] Under the FETAC Rules arbitration could occur before FETAC only if the parties had agreed to submit their dispute to arbitration. Such an agreement foreclosed the possibility of litigating the dispute in the Chinese judicial system, as Chinese Courts lacked jurisdiction over foreign economic and commercial matters in which the disputants had an agreement to submit their dispute to arbitration.[8] After a claimant submitted a request for arbitration to FETAC, the respondent was notified and required to return a defense statement. Counterclaims could also be submitted. The parties selected arbitrators appointed by CCPIT, all of whom were Chinese nationals. Hearings were held in open sessions and parties had the option of being represented by their authorized agents. Decisions were reached by majority vote immediately after the arbitration tribunal concluded the hearing, but were not subject to appeal. In the event that the award was not executed voluntarily, a petition could be submitted to the People's Court for enforcement.

In June 1988 the CCPIT, acting upon the approval of the State Council, renamed FETAC the China International Economic and Trade Arbitration Commission (hereafter CIETAC) and provided CIETAC with a new set of arbitral rules.[9] The CIETAC Rules clarified the jurisdiction of CIETAC by authorizing it to hear only disputes arising in the areas of international economics and trade.[10] On the other hand CIETAC's jurisdiction was broadened to enable it to hear disputes in which no Chinese parties are involved.[11] Furthermore, CIETAC was provided authority to rule on the validity of the arbitration agreement entered into between the parties as well as to determine its own jurisdiction over the case.[12]

Under the CIETAC Rules arbitration proceedings are commenced in a manner similar to the former FETAC Rules. The claimant submits an arbitration application, complete with supporting factual documentation, and appoints an arbitrator from CIETAC. CIETAC then notices the respondent, who has twenty days to appoint an arbitrator and forty-five days to file a defense statement and counterclaim, if any. Article 13 of the CIETAC Rules provides that on request of one of the parties, CIETAC may request a Chinese court to take steps to preserve the assets of the other party, presumably by ordering them not to be transferred or otherwise disposed of.

The pool of eligible CIETAC arbitrators was expanded to include foreigners—twelve initially, and the list has recently been expanded yet again. After each of the parties has appointed, or requested the CIETAC chair to appoint, an arbitrator from the panel, the chair will appoint the presiding arbitrator, thereby forming a three-person tribunal. Alternatively, the parties may appoint jointly one arbitrator. Either party may request an arbitrator with a conflict of interest to withdraw, but ultimate discretion to withdraw an arbitrator rests with the CIETAC chair.[13] During the hearing, the parties are to present evidence in support of the facts set forth in their claim or defense. The arbitration tribunal is empowered to undertake its own investigations and collect evidence. Unless both parties request otherwise, the hearing is held in private, although the tribunal is required to maintain a hearing record.

As with earlier arbitration practice, the CIETAC Rules permit the parties to engage in conciliation at any stage of the proceedings.[14] In the event a case is resolved through conciliation or mediation, CIETAC will issue an arbitral award in conformance with the contents of the conciliation agreement entered into between the parties. In a departure from the FETAC Rules, the arbitration tribunal may take up to forty-five days from the close of examination and hearing to issue its decision. In practice this often entails delays of several years. A decision issued by CIETAC is final and binding, and parties are not permitted to litigate any aspect of the same dispute resolved through arbitration. The arbitral award issued by CIETAC may be enforced through an Intermediate People's Court in accordance with the Civil Procedure Code if the award is not voluntarily executed by the losing party within the time limit prescribed in the award.[15]

Although most arbitration involving Chinese entities has taken place before CIETAC or its predecessor institutions, Chinese parties, in accordance with the contents of their arbitration clause or agreement, have engaged in arbitration before the Stockholm Chamber of Commerce, the London Court of International Arbitration, and the Hong Kong International Arbitration Center. However, there were doubts as to whether foreign arbitral awards would be enforced by China's judicial system. After China acceded to the New York Convention on the Recognition and Enforcement of Foreign Arbitral Awards, Chinese courts are bound to recognize and enforce foreign awards pursuant to the procedures set forth in the Convention.[16]

CIETAC's rules have once again been revised effective June 1, 1994.[17] The new rules now address provisions such as jurisdiction over contractual and non-contractual disputes; severability of the arbitral agreement; matters of waiver and estoppel in regards to the duty of a party to protest a violation of arbitral rules during the course of proceedings; duty of arbitrators to disclose their interests in particular cases; and the deemed incorporation of the new rules into the parties' arbitration agreement. The 1994 CIETAC-amended rules reflect the Commission's continued efforts to learn from international arbitration practice.

B. The Chinese Court System

The structure of China's judicial system is set forth in the Organic Law of the People's Courts.[18] The Supreme People's Court is the highest judicial body within the Chinese court system and has jurisdiction to hear cases of national importance and appeals from lower courts. It is composed of a president, elected by the National People's Congress, several vice presidents, and one chief and several associate judges, each of which is appointed by the Standing Committee of the National People's Congress. Immediately below the Supreme People's Court are the twenty-nine Higher People's Courts, one for each province, major municipality, and autonomous region. Each of the Higher People's Courts has authority to hear civil and criminal cases that affect the region over which the branch has jurisdiction, as well as appeals from Intermediate People's Courts in the region. The Intermediate People's Courts have original and appellate jurisdiction over cases within their district, which include the lowest level court called the Local or Basic People's Court. Special courts exist for matters pertaining to the military and other selected issues such as railroads and forestry. Beginning in 1979 economic tribunals were established in all levels of the People's Courts to hear cases involving contract disputes, foreign trade matters, and economic administrative matters such as patent violations. The economic tribunal in an Intermediate People's Court is the forum where cases involving foreigners are first heard.

The procedural rules for civil litigation in the People's Courts are set forth in the Civil Procedure Law of the People's Republic of China (hereafter CPL), which became effective in April 1991, thereby replacing the Draft Civil Procedure Law of 1982.[19] The CPL details rules concerning service of process, the taking of evidence, the conduct of the trial, and other pertinent matters relating to the trial and appeal of a civil suit, as well as the enforcement of arbitral awards. The CPL provides that all courts are to "exercise judicial power independently and are not subject to interference by administrative organs, public organizations or individuals."[20] The CPL contains specific provisions on the procedures to be used in civil actions involving foreign parties.[21] In a noteworthy departure from the provisional rules issued in 1982, the CPL eliminated the requirement of mandatory mediation. As noted earlier, disputes that are not subject to an arbitration agreement may be submitted for adjudication.

Recognition and Enforcement of Arbitral Awards

Although most commercial disputes involving a foreign party are unlikely to be tried before a Chinese court, Chinese courts do become involved in the recognition and enforcement of arbitral awards involving foreign parties rendered by CIETAC and by foreign arbitral tribunals.

CIETAC Arbitral Awards. To enforce an arbitral award issued by CIETAC, the prevailing party petitions the Intermediate People's Court in the district where the arbitral body is located or where the assets or residence of the losing party are situated. Under Article 260 of the CPL the arbitral award is not enforceable if the losing party can assert successfully one or more of the following defenses: (1) no arbitration agreement was entered into between the parties; (2) the arbitration agreement was invalid; (3) notice of the arbitration proceeding was not served or served improperly; (4) there was a fatal defect in the arbitration proceedings; or (5) the arbitration institution had no authority to issue the award. Furthermore, People's Courts will not enforce an award if it is determined to be against the social and public interest of China. In the event that an award is found to be unenforceable, the parties may arbitrate their dispute again or litigate the matter.[22]

Foreign Arbitral Awards. Before China joined the New York Convention in 1986, enforcement of foreign arbitral awards in China was problematic.[23] Attempts were made to include guarantee clauses in bilateral treaties that would increase the likelihood of enforcement, although the requirement of adherence to local law often hindered this prospect.[24] As China has now acceded to the New York Convention,[25] an award made by a foreign arbitral tribunal may be enforced in China pursuant to the procedures of the Convention if the foreign tribunal is located in a country that is a signatory to the Convention. Shortly before the New York Convention became effective in China, the Supreme People's Court distributed a document to Intermediate People's Courts throughout the country, providing instructions on the implementation of the Convention and explanations with respect to China's reservations.[26]

China's accession to the New York Convention is subject to reciprocity and commercial reservations.[27] Under the reciprocity reservation China will recognize and enforce an arbitral award pursuant to the New York Convention only if it is made by an arbitration institution in another contracting state. Arbitral awards issued by institutions in noncontracting states are to be recognized and enforced in accordance with the CPL. Under the commercial reservation, China will recognize and enforce foreign awards only if they arise from contractual or noncontractual legal relationships that are commercial in nature, such as the purchase and sale of goods; leasing of property; contracts for projects and processing; technology transfer; equity, cooperative, and natural resource joint ventures; insurance; loans and credits; and selected other services, but *not* including disputes between foreign investors and the government of China.

II. Performance of the Foreign Dispute Resolution System

The first fifteen years of reform following 1978 saw a dramatic expansion in the frequency of commercial disputes involving China's foreign economic relations.[28] The preference of foreign businesses clearly has been for arbitral resolution rather than court litigation, as is the case with international business disputes unrelated to China, and by the early 1990s, CIETAC's case load was averaging one hundred cases per year.[29]

Even though the "Foreign Economic Litigation Chambers" (*shewai jingji shenpan ting*) of the Chinese People's Courts are available to hear disputes involving foreign parties, foreign disputants have largely avoided participating in court litigation if possible. The Chinese courts are seen as being heavily politicized. This perception is influenced significantly by the continued role of the Communist Party-dominated "adjudication committees" despite an official directive ordering a diminution in their activities.[30] Also, the exclusion of foreign lawyers from direct participation in court proceedings and their inability even to secure membership in the Chinese bar association confirm foreign businesses' doubts about the likelihood of receiving a fair hearing. Thus, the politicization, low level of professionalism, and local protectionism of the Chinese courts[31] have largely made the courts inadequate to address effectively the dispute resolution concerns of foreign businesses, and most foreign businesses avoid them where possible. However, foreign businesses have little choice in the matter of enforcement of arbitral awards where the Chinese courts play a pivotal role.

A. Arbitration Proceedings

Virtually all Chinese standard form contracts call for resolution of disputes before CIETAC or some other Chinese institution. Often this is presented as a requirement, whereas in fact under the Foreign Economic Contract Law the situs of dispute resolution remains a matter for agreement between the parties. Although foreign lawyers generally advise against electing to arbitrate in China, the general consensus is also that the arbitration results at CIETAC at least are generally fair and generally reach the "correct" results, even if often for the wrong reasons. Foreign lawyers may participate directly on behalf of their foreign clients,[32] and the CIETAC list of arbitrators available to be selected to decide a given case contains a number of respected foreign jurists.[33] Indeed, some studies have shown that CIETAC decisions favor the foreign side more often than not.[34] CIETAC is relatively internationalized and keenly interested in maintaining its international reputation. This encourages attention to process that might otherwise be lacking elsewhere among Chinese government agencies.

However, many foreign lawyers who have experience handling disputes in China have noted a number of problems. The first concerns difficulties in securing assistance in obtaining evidence in China. Although a wide variety of evidence may usually be brought before an arbitral tribunal,[35] often relevant evidence—whether physical or in the form of testimony—cannot be obtained without the cooperation of local Chinese courts and notarial officials. Chinese arbitration organs are seen as unable and often unwilling to assist disputants in obtaining this evidence: The influence of arbitral organs over local courts is minimal, and they are reluctant to reveal this by issuing requests for judicial assistance that are likely to be dismissed or ignored.[36] The difficulties in obtaining evidence in China for use in Chinese arbitration proceedings are compounded by the fact that as yet China has not joined the UN Convention on Collection of Evidence Abroad, thus underscoring the problems of obtaining evidence in China for use in either domestic or foreign proceedings.

A second area of concern has been the lack of adequate staff. Staff work in arbitral proceedings can extend to legal research, preparation of bench memos on issues of fact and law, and handling the myriad of administrative correspondence. In each of these areas, the arbitral commissions in China are generally seen to lack adequate staffing—both in numbers and in the level of training. However, it should be noted that CIETAC and its companion arbitral organs elsewhere in China have attempted to address this issue by recruiting top law students and also by arranging foreign training for their staff. Nonetheless, staffing remains a problem that augments the difficulties in collecting evidence. In essence, the culture and approach taken by CIETAC and its companion organs in emphasizing fairness are to a certain extent undermined by difficulties related to evidentiary collection and the staffing necessary for in-depth juridical analysis and smooth administration.

A final area of concern involves enforcement. CIETAC and its companion organs do not have authority on their own to enforce arbitral decisions. This rests with the courts. But as discussed in the next section, judicial enforcement is problematic, thus undermining the limited gains made by the Chinese arbitration system.

B. Judicial Recognition and Enforcement

Although Chinese courts are bound under the New York Convention to recognize and enforce, subject to the Convention's procedural requirements, arbitral decisions reached outside of China, unfortunately, the few proceedings that have been attempted to date in China have not met with great success. And indeed, the record indicates that Chinese courts have tended to refuse recognition on grounds unrelated to the New York Convention. Local protectionism, budgetary constraints, procedural complexities, and staffing problems have all played a role in impeding judicial recognition and enforcement.[37]

The enforcement of CIETAC awards has also been problematic. The 1991 revisions to the Civil Procedure Law of the PRC required plaintiffs seeking to enforce arbitral awards to file suit at the intermediate-level People's Court in the location of the Chinese defendant (rather than in Beijing, where the arbitral tribunal was located as under the previous rule).[38] This has increased the potential for local protectionism to interfere with the smooth enforcement of arbitral awards rendered in China and abroad.

It appears clear that, unlike the arbitral tribunals in China whose internationalism and commitment to independence have permitted results attentive to basic fairness despite infrastructural problems, the courts in general have neither the institutional or staffing strength nor the internationalism and commitment to fairness to litigants that characterize the arbitral courts. Although many individual judges are committed to improving the work of the courts in international proceedings, the record as far as enforcement of arbitral awards is concerned is not good. In effect, China remains unable to assure foreign businesses that their arbitral awards, whether received from Chinese or foreign arbitral institutions, will be enforced by Chinese courts.

III. Attitudes Affecting Performance of the System

The performance of China's foreign dispute resolution system is affected by a number of conflicting attitudinal issues. These entail the conceptual separation of foreign and domestic matters, as well as the interplay between Communist Party influence and local parochialism.

The extent to which CCPIT and CIETAC have been successful in building an arbitration system that has at least the appearance of impartiality is largely the result of the conceptual separation of foreign and domestic law. Operating in what once was a carefully demarcated arena of foreign economic law, CIETAC's internationalism was seen as necessary for an institution whose primary function involved dealing with foreigners. Thus, resorting to foreign and international law was tolerated because these were the basis for the international trade relations in which China wished to participate. Foreign training and travel for arbitrators and staff were justified under the same rationale.

But this was a conflicted approach, which often faced challenges on political and ideological grounds that were more concerned with domestic China than China's international relationships and concepts. Indeed, it was not until 1987 that CIETAC decided to include foreigners on its panel of arbitrators, and this development itself was tied clearly to China's accession to the New York Convention. Yet many officials within CIETAC were known to have urged the inclusion of foreign arbitrators and the accession to the New York Convention earlier, but were stymied by political pressures concerned with maintaining China's separation and independence from the effects of international capitalism.

If these pressures affected the gradual internationalization of CIETAC, they were felt more fully in the court system. The very presence of the distinct chambers for handling foreign disputes separately from domestic ones reveals the attitudinal commitment to the separation of foreign and domestic matters that is reflected elsewhere in the legal system. Legal procedures and substantive law are not seen as being generally applicable to foreigners and local Chinese alike, but rather must be tailored specifically according to the circumstances of the parties' nationality. Moreover, Chinese approaches to international judicial cooperation reflect concerns over protecting local interests. Thus, China acceded to the UN Convention on Service Abroad of Judicial and Extrajudicial Documents in Civil or Commercial Matters,[39] which might be useful in bringing foreign parties before Chinese courts, but has not so far acceded to the UN Convention on Collection of Evidence Abroad,[40] which might commit Chinese institutions to cooperate with intrusive fact collection by foreign lawyers.

In addition, the courts' general lack of internationalization stems from the political system in which they operate. Despite efforts in the mid-1950s to formalize the court system, Maoist ideology denied a significant role for the courts in general.[41] The functions of the courts are also weakened by their organizational position as components of the administrative bureaucracy.[42] This undermined the courts' authority and made such supervisory authority, as was granted politically, difficult to exercise. The continued dominance of the Chinese Communist Party in court decision making has permitted local political interests to take priority in adjudication of disputes. This permits the phenomenon of so-called local protectionism to emerge, by which local political interests hamper judicial cooperation between provinces in China and also impede enforcement of local court decisions.[43]

The conflict between the internationalism of the Chinese arbitral organs and the parochialism of the courts present obstacles to the full development of a foreign dispute resolution system in China. For without the enforcement powers of the courts, arbitral decisions, domestic and foreign alike, are rendered moot. Unfortunately cooperation between arbitral and judicial organs seems increasingly remote, as indicated by the vigorous debate concerning the role of judicial review as a prerequisite for enforcement of CIETAC and international arbitral awards in connection with the revised Civil Procedure Law. By insisting that the review authority of the Chinese People's Courts be extended beyond the purely domestic arbitration cases handled by the State Administration of Industry and Commerce to include CIETAC cases and also cases heard by foreign tribunals, the judiciary may have exacerbated the tensions between China's arbitral and judicial organs. It appeared to many observers that this debate was more about politics and institutional authority than about law and legal process. This underscored for some observers the continued tension between the political parochialism of the Chinese court system and the internationalized CIETAC arbitration system.

IV. Implications

The institutions and procedures for the resolution of disputes involving foreign parties in China have developed dramatically over the past fifteen years. Significant increases in the extent and range of economic disputes have given rise to a host of new laws on organization and procedures. Foreign business parties in China have benefited from these changes, as the availability of arbitral or even judicial recourse has affected negotiating attitudes and commercial practices. Yet, in spite of the impressive development of China's dispute resolution system, problems remain. These are primarily infrastructural in the case of the arbitration system whereas in the case of the judiciary they are attitudinal as well. Thus, significant barriers remain to the fair and effective handling of disputes involving foreign business in China. The real and perceived deficiencies with China's foreign dispute resolution system have a chilling effect on the potential for expansion in the size and complexity of foreign business activities. Many business executives are simply unwilling to expand their activities in China unless and until improvements are made in the integrity and expertise of the institutions and personnel involved in foreign dispute resolution.

CHAPTER 7

Conclusions and Proposals for Further Reform

The Chinese legal system governing foreign economic relations has made significant achievements since its inception in 1978. As indicated by Appendix A, the wealth of legislative and regulatory enactments alone would suggest a vigorous effort to establish a legal foundation for foreign business activities. In contrast to the relative dearth of regulatory enactments that greeted foreign business executives and their counselors in the early 1980s, a full array of laws and regulations is now in place. Many of these have been aimed specifically at encouraging foreign investment in China. And indeed, China's foreign business relations have shown significant growth over the past decade and a half. Although there are doubts about the existence of a causal relationship between law and foreign business,[1] the 1980s have nonetheless witnessed a significant growth in foreign business as well as a marked expansion of the regulatory regime.[2]

I. Tensions Between Chinese Approaches and Foreign Business Concerns

Despite these developments, foreign business executives place the regulatory environment high on their list of complaints about the business climate in China.[3] A discussion of the content and performance of the legal regimes governing selected aspects of China's foreign business relations and of the attitudes that affect performance suggest that the goals guiding Chinese regulatory efforts are at odds with the main concerns of foreign business.

Instrumentalism dominates the regulatory regimes, and permits them to be subordinated to policy and attendant domestic ideological and political conflicts. Under such conditions doctrinal consistency is difficult to obtain and this

81

in turn undermines predictability. Formalistic approaches to the performance of the legal system make meaningful improvements difficult. Assumptions that the policy and doctrinal precepts articulated through law and regulation are actually enforced in practice tend to inhibit reform. In specific areas, other problems exist as well, such as tendencies toward mercantilism in trade policy; ineffective attention to market concerns in investment incentives; the culture of secrecy that impedes the free flow of information and undermines transparency; the culture of emulation and antidependency that poses obstacles to intellectual property protection; the tensions between concerns over revenue and the need to induce foreign business that affects the performance of the financial system; and the tension between internationalism and parochialism that characterized the dispute resolution system. Yet these tend to be exacerbated by basic philosophies of instrumentalism and formalism that underlie the Chinese legal system as a whole.

In such an environment, legislative initiatives for foreign business can only be incremental and limited, as such initiatives remain the product of policy debate and political compromise over issues that have little if anything to do with foreign business concerns. Foreign business operators are generally concerned with systemic issues, such as predictability and transparency in regulatory behavior as well as underlying policy. Recognizing that the Chinese state is unlikely to meet these objectives in the near term, many foreign business operators would be content with a regulatory system that relied on market forces, which might lend some stability to legal rules.

II. Systemic Reforms

The contradictions between the Chinese government's approaches to the regulation of foreign economic relations and the objectives and concerns of foreign business frequently undercut the commendable efforts of Chinese reformers to improve the business climate. A possible approach to resolving these tensions would be to reach broad agreement on general approaches to business regulation. This would entail emphasizing systemic principles as opposed to narrowly conceived instrumentalist measures: Transparency and predictability in policy making and regulatory enforcement would be emphasized over functional topics for government regulation. Where narrow measures are required, the emphasis should be on market-oriented approaches. However, these should be based on the identification and manipulation of practical market mechanisms, rather than on imprecise notions of broad-based deregulation.

Institutional reforms should also be discussed that focus on transparency in policy- and law-making processes. This would entail the establishment of procedures by which foreign business concerns could provide meaningful input without fear of bureaucratic retribution. A system of administrative hearings might be a useful start to the establishment of a process by which regulation would be the product of dialogue among relevant sectors of the administrative system and the economy. Unified legislative processes might also be considered, including the extensive use of technical amendments to ensure that regulations and laws emerging from different sectors of the Chinese bureaucracy are consistent with one another. Finally, the judicial review system begun with the ALL would be expanded and improved, such that foreign business has meaningful opportunities to challenge regulations and administrative rulings. This would entail expanding the reach of the ALL and enacting additional measures that permit effective review of not only administrative decisions but also underlying rules and regulations.

Although the institutional and attitudinal obstacles to many of these reforms are acute, they should not distract from efforts at systemic reforms intended to meaningfully change the regulatory framework governing China's foreign economic relations. Indeed, numerous discussions with Chinese lawyers and legal scholars, regulatory officials, and political leaders have convinced this author that many of these proposals are not only possible but have been specifically contemplated by decisionmakers within the Chinese political elite. These suggestions for systemic reform are offered with the certain knowledge that they are consonant with the views of many Chinese reformers and are already on the agenda for constructive change.

III. Reforms in Individual Topic Areas

In addition to the systemic reforms already suggested, specific reforms would be appropriate in each of the individual topic areas under discussion.

A. Trade Relations

Regulatory reform in the trade area should begin with removing barriers to trade. The Sino-U.S. Market Access Agreement articulated a number of useful principles, but more are needed. Additional reforms might include the following:

- The commodity inspection system might usefully be rationalized so that standards are publicly available and subject to judicial review. This will benefit both China and its foreign trade partners by removing a major stumbling block to China's accession to the GATT.

- Reforms in the import and export licensing system might also be considered that emphasize market factors and condition the issuance and scope of licenses on the nature of the products involved rather than the organizational identity of the Chinese exporters and import end users.
- Customs procedures might usefully be reformed to clarify the conditions for calculation of import duties and the underlying duty value of imported goods. This might entail not only greater specificity in the calculation standards, but also greater transparency in the processes involved.

B. Foreign Investment

Reforms in the investment area center on policy stability and market orientation. These in turn require the emergence of a genuine and lasting consensus among Chinese policymakers as to the benefits of foreign investment in China. Based on such consensus, policies might be enacted with assurances as to their duration. In the absence of firm commitments, policy statements articulating the factors that are to govern the policy process would be useful.

Market-oriented policies are critical to the investment climate in China. This does not mean simply that the state withdraw from all regulatory activity, but rather that it use its regulatory power to encourage activities that are healthy for a diverse economy. Specific reforms might include the following:

- Tentative steps toward expanding the permitted scope for certain types of activities such as the organization of investment-holding companies; energy consortia; and long-distance transportation conglomerates should be encouraged and expanded.
- Further reduction of barriers to investment in selected areas of the Chinese economy such as telecommunications, transportation, insurance, finance, and banking.
- Formalistic distinctions between foreign representative offices and foreign investment enterprises might be reconsidered.
- A meaningful commitment to building infrastructure might usefully be considered.

C. Technology Transfer

The single most important reforms in the technology transfer area involve protection of intellectual property rights. The enactment of a foundation of laws and regulations for the protection of patents, copyrights, and trademarks is a commendable start, but it is inadequate and indeed irrelevant without effective enforcement. Effective enforcement of intellectual property rights will require a difficult commitment of political capital in an effort to counteract the forces of tradition, ideology, and the pursuit of short-term gain. However, this is fundamentally in China's long-term interests since, in the absence of meaningful protection, foreign technology owners simply will not be willing to transfer their most valuable properties to China. Domestic technology developers as well will be less than eager to develop and market new products. Specific reforms might include:

- Amendment or supplementation of existing intellectual property laws to emphasize punitive sanctions and effective cease and desist orders backed up by sanctions as a first step toward encouraging compliance with existing laws.
- Permitting administrative organs to issue sanctions that, subject to judicial review under the ALL, may be enforced directly by the public security authorities without the need for enforcement litigation. This would permit enforcement agencies to begin to work effectively to curb the widespread violations of intellectual property rights.
- Permitting and encouraging the courts to impose effective penalties on violators would be an additional useful step.

D. Finance

Reforms in the finance aspects of foreign business regulation might focus on resolving the tension between the pursuit of short-term financial gains and the ongoing need to create a stable finance environment.

Existing reforms in the foreign exchange area should be encouraged and expanded, including:

- Permit the establishment of an effective interbank market for foreign exchange and reduce or eliminate arbitrary government intervention in the sale and circulation of foreign exchange in the interbank market.
- Ensure that foreign investment enterprises have access to their bank foreign currency accounts without government interference. Finalize and make transparent the procedures by which FIEs access their foreign exchange deposits.

In the area of taxation, possible reforms might include the following:

- Expansion of existing inducements to give greater weight to the character of investments rather than their location. Thus preferences for advanced technology enterprises and export-oriented enterprises might be brought to par with those available for investments in the Special Economic Zones and Economic and Technology Development Zones. Additional induce-

ments might be considered in areas of infrastructural development such as transportation and energy.
- Effective measures should be aimed at eliminating the multitude of informal taxes and fees levied against foreign businesses.
- Increased procedural regularity should be established for tax calculation and enforcement, including effective opportunities for seeking judicial review.

E. Dispute Resolution

Reforms in the area of dispute resolution should focus on encouraging closer cooperation between the judicial and arbitration systems so as to improve the content and enforcement of judgments and arbitral awards. These might usefully include:
- Judicial cooperation in collection of evidence for use in arbitral proceedings and in enforcement of arbitral awards.
- Stronger budgetary commitments to both arbitral organs and courts in order to improve staffing.
- Stronger support for cooperation between Chinese and foreign arbitral bodies in order to provide training and experience for staff lawyers and arbitrators.
- Better international cooperation in exchange of ideas and information for use in the evolving regimes for dispute resolution.
- Specific legislative initiatives that clarify in detail the obligations of courts to enforce foreign arbitral awards and the processes to be used. Until the Chinese courts demonstrate a better record on the enforcement of arbitral awards, I would not suggest that they be given power to amend arbitral awards at present, although this might be contemplated for a future in which Chinese courts have achieved a modicum of independent professionalism.

* * *

This volume has attempted to describe the existing condition of the regulatory regimes governing China's foreign economic relations, assess their performance and the attitudinal bases for such performance, and suggest reforms that might usefully be considered to address the concerns raised. It is noted that the current (1993–94) round of economic reform policies reflect some appreciation of the points raised herein. This book is not intended to second-guess the ongoing reform process in China. Rather it is hoped that this effort may promote further discussion and analysis that will ultimately contribute to China assuming its rightful place as a full member of the world economy.

It is recognized that many of the reforms suggested here derive from Western theories on the interaction between legal institutions and economic development, theories that have not yet found their way securely into the Chinese view of the relationships among and between the state, the economy, and society. In addition, the implementation of the suggested reforms of necessity would move China away from values and practices that are embedded in centuries of Chinese tradition, which have survived today in the China of the People's Republic. Thus, the reforms will surely be difficult to implement and some may not be capable of implementation in the near term. Yet, despite the transformations in culture and institutions that these reforms would require and to which they have to be linked in order to become meaningful, it is believed that China needs to move toward the goals suggested here if it wishes to provide an appropriate institutional framework and environment for foreign trade and investment. The initial enthusiasm demonstrated by the manifest increase in foreign investment in China may not survive in the long term if reforms prove to lack substance. It is obviously the province of the people and government of the People's Republic to determine what balance they find acceptable between maintenance of traditional values and cultural systems on the one hand and increased and sustained foreign investment and trade on the other. Striking this balance will most certainly require time and will continue to affect legal reform in the People's Republic.

APPENDIX A

List of Laws
and Regulations Cited*

Chapter 1. Introduction

Economic Contract Law of the PRC (1981, 1993), in CCH, para. 5–500.

Foreign Economic Contract Law of the PRC (1985), in CCH, para. 5–550.

General Principles of Civil Law of the PRC (1986), in CCH, para. 19–150.

Administrative Litigation Law of the PRC (1989), in CCH, para. 19–558.

Law of the PRC on the Protection of Taiwan Compatriots' Investment (1994), in *China Economic News*, Mar. 21, 1994, p. 6.

Chapter 2. Foreign Trade

General Agreement On Tariffs and Trade (1947, as amended) TIAS 1700, 55 U.N.T.S. 187, IV GATT Basic Instrument and Selected Documents [BISD], Article XXIV.

Provisional Regulations Governing the Export License System of the Administrative Commission on Import and Export and the Ministry of Foreign Trade (1980), in CCH, para. 51–500.

Details Concerning the Export License System Governing Eleven Categories of Export Commodities (1982), in CCH, para. 51–520.

Interim Regulations on the Import Commodities Licensing System of the PRC (1984), in CCH, para. 51–600.

Regulations of the PRC on the Inspection of Imported and Exported Goods (1984), in CCH, para. 16–600.

Foreign Economic Contract Law of the PRC (1985), in CCH, para. 5–550.

State Council Regulations for the Encouragement of Foreign Investment (1986), in CCH, para. 13–509.

Ministry of Foreign Economic Relations and Trade Methods on the Purchase and Export of Domestic Products by Foreign Business Enterprises to Balance Income and Expenditures of Foreign Exchange (1987), in CCH, para. 13–526.

Customs Law of the PRC (1987), in CCH, para. 50–300.

*The materials cited in this Appendix are presented in chronological order. Unless otherwise indicated, all citations are to CCH Australia Ltd., *China Laws for Foreign Business* (looseleaf). Citation will be to "CCH, para . . .".

Measures Relating to the Import Substitution by Products Manufactured by Chinese-Foreign Equity Joint Ventures and Chinese-Foreign Cooperative Ventures (1987), in CCH, para. 50–653.

Implementing Regulations for the Quality License System for Imported Electrical and Mechanical Commodities (for Trial Use) (1990), in CCH, para. 51–620.

People's Republic of China-United States Memorandum of Understanding Concerning Market Access (1992), in *International Legal Materials*, vol. 31, p. 1274 (1992).

"Speed Up the Pace of Reform, Opening, and Modernization and Win Greater Victories in the Socialist Cause With Chinese Characteristics," Jiang Zemin report to the Fourteenth CPC National Congress, Oct. 12, 1992, in *FBIS Daily Report-China: Supplement*, Oct. 21, 1992, esp. pp. 12–13.

"Final Version of 14th CPC National Congress Report," in *FBIS Daily Report-China*, Oct. 21, 1992, p. 1.

North American Free Trade Agreement (Final Text), Dec. 17, 1992 (CCH International, 1992).

Foreign Trade Law of the PRC (1994), in *China Economic News*, May 23, 1994, p. 8, May 30, 1994, p. 7.

Chapter 3. Foreign Investment

Charter of Economic Rights and Duties of States (UN GA Resolution 3281 [XXIX], Dec. 12, 1974).

Joint Venture Law of the PRC (1980, rev. 1990) in CCH, para. 6–500.

Interim Regulations Concerning the Control of Resident Offices of Foreign Enterprises (1980), in CCH, para. 7–500.

Constitution of the People's Republic of China (1982, rev. 1993), in CCH, para. 4–500.

Regulations of the People's Republic of China on the Exploitation of Offshore Petroleum Resources in Cooperation with Foreign Enterprises (1982), in CCH, para. 14–560.

Procedures of the People's Bank of China for the Establishment of Representative Offices in China by Overseas and Foreign Financial Institutions (1983), in CCH, para. 7–540(4).

Implementing Regulations for the Joint Venture Law of the PRC (1983, rev. 1986), in CCH, para. 6–550.

Provisional Regulations of the PRC State Council Concerning Reduction and Elimination of Enterprise Tax and Industrial and Commercial Consolidated Tax in the Special Economic Zones and 14 Coastal Cities (1984), in CCH, para. 70–845.

Foreign Economic Contract Law of the PRC (1985), in CCH, para. 5–550.

Law of the PRC on Enterprises Operated Exclusively with Foreign Capital (1986), in CCH, para. 13–506.

State Council Measures for the Encouragement of Foreign Investment (1986), in CCH, para. 13–509.

Municipal Regulations on Encouraging Foreign Investment for Beijing, in *Beijing ribao*, Nov. 16, 1986, p. 2.

Municipal Regulations on Encouraging Foreign Investment for Shanghai, in *Wenhui bao*, Oct. 25, 1986.

Implementing Regulations for the State Council Measures for the Encouragement of Foreign Investment (all in *Zhongguo guli wai shang touze fagui xuanbian* [Compilation of laws and regulations of China on encouraging foreign investment] [Beijing: University of Politics and Law Press, 1987]):

1. Labor Ministry Regulations Concerning Autonomy in the Hiring of Personnel and in Salaries, Insurance and Expenses, Welfare Funds of Foreign Investment Enterprises (Nov. 26, 1986);
2. PRC Customs Methods for Administration of Materials and Things Imported by Foreign Investment Enterprises as Needed to Fulfill Goods Export Contracts (Nov. 24, 1986);
3. Bank of China Methods for Loans of Renminbi Secured by Foreign Exchange (Dec. 11, 1986);
4. MOFERT Methods on the Purchase and Export of Domestic Products by Foreign Investment Enterprises to Balance Income and Expenditures of Foreign Exchange (Jan. 20, 1987);
5. MOFERT Implementing Procedures for Applications by Foreign Investment Enterprises for Import and Export Licenses (Jan. 24, 1987);
6. MOFERT Implementing Rules for Examination and Confirmation of Export Enterprises and Technologically Advanced Enterprises with Foreign Investment (Jan. 27, 1987), also in *China Economic News*, Nov. 7, 1987, p. 9;
7. Ministry of Finance Procedures for Implementation of Tax Preferences Contained in the State Council Provisions for the Encouragement of Foreign Investment (Jan. 30, 1987);
8. Bank of China Methods for Loans to Foreign Investment Enterprises (Apr. 4, 1987);
9. State Planning Commission Measures Relating to Import Substitution by Products Manufactured by Sino-Foreign Joint Ventures (Oct. 1987);
10. State Economic Commission Measures Relating to Substitution of Mechanical and Electrical Products Manufactured by Sino-Foreign Joint Ventures (Oct. 1987).

Provincial Measures on Encouraging Foreign Investment Enacted in Fujian, Shandong, Liaoning, Guizhou, Jiangsu, Heilongjiang, Jilin, Yunnan, Guangxi, and Guangdong Provinces appear in *Zhongguo guli wai shang touze fagui xuanbian* (Compilation of laws and regulations of China on encouraging foreign investment) (Beijing: University of Politics and Law Press, 1987), at pp. 159–195.

Municipal Regulations for Encouraging Foreign Investment for Guangzhou, in *China Economic News*, July 6, 1987, p. 5, July 13, 1987, p. 7, and July 20, 1987, p. 9.

Law of the People's Republic of China on Sino-Foreign Cooperative Enterprises (1988), in CCH, para. 6–100.

Shanghai Municipality, Sino-Foreign Equity Joint Venture Labor Union Regulations (1989), in *China Law and Practice*, Feb. 26, 1990, p. 52.

National People's Congress Revision of the PRC Sino-Foreign Equity Joint Venture Law Decision," para. 3 (re: JV Law Article 6), in *China Law and Practice*, May 7, 1990, p. 36.

Implementing Rules for the Law of the PRC on Wholly Foreign-Owned Enterprises (1990), in CCH, para. 13–507.

Procedures of the People's Bank of China for Controls Relating to Establishment of Representative Offices in China by Foreign Banking Institutions (1991), in CCH, para. 7–542.

Supplement to Implementary Rules of MOFERT for Examination and Confirmation of

Export Enterprises and Technologically Advanced Enterprises With Foreign Investment (1992), in *China Economic News*, Nov. 19, 1992, p. 7.

Regulations of the PRC on Sino-Foreign Cooperation in the Development of Continental Petroleum Resources (1993), in *China Economic News*, Nov. 15, 1993, p. 7.

Company Law of the PRC (1993), in *China Economic News*, Supplement no. 2, March 7, 1994.

Regulations of the PRC on the Management of Foreign-Funded Financial Institutions (1994), in *China Economic News*, Apr. 18, 1994, p. 6.

Chapter 4. Technology Transfer

Berne Convention on the Protection of Literary and Artistic Works (1886, as amended 1971), Article 18(1), WIPO Doc. 287(E).

Paris Convention for the Protection of Industrial Property, in *International Legal Materials*, vol. 6, p. 981 (1968).

Agreement on Trade Relations Between the U.S.A. and P.R.C. (1979), in 31 U.S.T. 4651.

Joint Venture Law of the PRC (1979, rev. 1990), in CCH., para. 6–500.

Constitution of the PRC (1982), in CCH, para. 4–500.

Provisional Regulations on Technology Transfer (1985), in CCH, para. 19–536.

United States 1988 Omnibus Trade and Competitiveness Act, 19 U.S.C. 2411–2416 (1982 & Supp. IV 1986).

Implementing Regulations for the Joint Venture Law of the PRC (1983, rev. 1986), in CCH, para. 6–550.

Trademark Law of the PRC (1983, rev. 1993), in CCH, para. 11–500.

Detailed Rules for the Implementation of the Trademark Law of the People's Republic of China (1983, rev. 1988), in CCH, para. 11–510.

Provisional Regulations on Technology Transfer (1985), in CCH, para. 19–536.

State Council Regulations on the Administration of Technology Import Contracts of the People's Republic of China (1985), in CCH, para. 5–570.

Regulations of the PRC Governing Trademarks (1963) (Shangbiao guanli tiaoli), in Trademark Office of the State Administration for Industry and Commerce, *Shangbiao fagui ziliao xuanbian* (Selected laws and regulations and materials on trademark) (Beijing: Law Publishers, 1985), p. 52.

Patent Law of the PRC (1985, rev. 1993), in CCH, para. 11–600.

Implementation Regulations for the Patent Law of the PRC (1985), in CCH, para. 11–603.

Law of the PRC on Enterprises Operated Exclusively with Foreign Capital (1986), in CCH, para. 13–506.

State Council Measures for the Encouragement of Foreign Investment (1986), in CCH, para. 13–509.

State Council Implementing Rules for the Confirmation and Examination of Export-Oriented and Technologically Advanced Enterprises with Foreign Investment (1987), in CCH, para. 13–530.

Law of the PRC on Technology Contracts (1987), in CCH, para 6–731.

Detailed Rules for the Implementation of the Administrative Regulations of the People's Republic of China on Technology Import Contracts (1987), in CCH, para. 5–573.

Law of the People's Republic of China on Sino-Foreign Cooperative Enterprises (1988), in CCH, para. 6–100.

Administrative Litigation Law of the PRC (1989), in CCH, para. 19–558.

Beijing Municipality Patent Dispute Mediation Procedures (1988), in *China Law and Practice*, Aug. 21, 1989, p. 54.

Shanghai Patent Dispute Mediation Tentative Procedures (1988), in *China Law and Practice*, Aug. 21, 1989, p. 59.

Memorandum of Understanding (MOU) between USTR and MOFERT (1989) (author's copy).

State Council Regulations for the Encouragement of Foreign Investment (1989), in CCH, para. 13–509.

Patent Administrative Authority Adjudicating Patent Disputes Procedures (1989), in *China Law and Practice*, May 7, 1990, p. 40.

Copyright Law of the PRC (1990), in CCH, para. 11–700.

Detailed Rules for the Implementation of the Copyright Law of the PRC (1991), in CCH, para. 11–702.

Computer Software Protection Regulations of the PRC (1991), in CCH, para. 11–704.

Memorandum of Understanding between the Government of the People's Republic of China and the Government of the United States of America on the Protection of Intellectual Property (1992) (author's copy).

Supplement to MOFERT Implementing Rules for Examination and Confirmation of Export Enterprises and Export-Oriented Enterprises (1992), in *China Economic News*, Nov. 19, 1992, p. 7.

Administrative Protection of Pharmaceutical Regulations (1993), in *China Law and Practice*, Mar. 25, 1993, p. 37.

White Paper on Intellectual Property (1994), in *FBIS Daily Report–China*, June 16, 1994, p. 32.

Berne Convention on the Protection of Literary and Artistic Works, Article 18(1), WIPO Doc. 287(E).

Chapter 5. Taxation and Foreign Exchange

Joint Venture Law of the PRC (1979, rev. 1990), in CCH, para. 6–500.

Individual Income Tax Law of the People's Republic of China (1980, 1993), in CCH, para. 30–500.

Income Tax Law of the PRC Concerning Joint Ventures with Chinese and Foreign Investment (1980), in *China's Foreign Economic Legislation Vol. I* (Beijing: Foreign Languages Press, 1982), pp. 36–44.

Detailed Rules for the Implementation of the Income Tax Law of the PRC for Joint Ventures with Chinese and Foreign Investment (1980) in *China's Foreign Economic Legislation Vol. I* (Beijing: Foreign Languages Press, 1982), pp. 45–55.

Foreign Enterprise Income Tax Law of the PRC (1981), in *China's Foreign Economic Legislation Vol. I* (Beijing: Foreign Languages Press, 1982), pp. 55–63.

Individual Income Tax Law of the People's Republic of China (1980) in *China's Foreign Economic Legislation Vol. I* (Beijing: Foreign Languages Press, 1982), p. 75.

Rules for the Implementation of the Individual Income Tax Law of the People's Republic of China, in *China's Foreign Economic Legislation Vol. I* (Beijing: Foreign Languages Press, 1982), p. 85.

Detailed Rules for the Implementation of the Foreign Enterprise Income Tax Law of the PRC (1982), in *China's Foreign Economic Legislation Vol. II* (Beijing: Foreign Languages Press, 1982), pp. 64–74.

Rules for the Implementation of Foreign Exchange Controls Relating to Enterprises with Overseas Chinese Capital, Enterprises with Foreign Capital, and Chinese-Foreign Equity Joint Ventures (1983), in CCH, para. 8–670.

Implementing Regulations for the Joint Venture Law of the PRC (1983, rev. 1986), in CCH, para. 6–550.

Provisional Regulations of the PRC State Council Concerning Reduction and Elimination of Enterprise Tax and Industrial and Commercial Consolidated Tax in the Special Economic Zones and 14 Coastal Cities (1984), in CCH, para. 70–845.

Shenzhen Special Economic Zone Supplemental Regulations on Reduction of Taxation on Enterprises (1986), in CCH, para. 73–527.

Regulations Concerning the Issue of Balancing Foreign Exchange Receipts and Disbursements by Joint Ventures Using Chinese and Foreign Investment (1986), in Dept. of Treaties and Law, Ministry of Foreign Economic Relations and Trade, *Collection of Laws and Regulations of the People's Republic of China Concerning Foreign Economic Affairs* (Beijing: Law Publishers, periodical), vol. 5, p. 106.

Draft Regulations of the PRC on Value-Added Tax (Zhonghua renmin gongheguo zengzhishui tiaoli) (1984) in Beijing Taxation Society and Beijing Economics Institute eds., *Na shui zixun shouce* (Handbook of consultation on payment of tax) (Beijing: Beijing Publishers, 1986), p. 561.

MOFERT Measures for Foreign Investment Enterprises Purchasing Domestic Products for Export to Achieve a Balance of Foreign Exchange Income and Expenditure (1987), in CCH, para. 13–526.

Measures Relating to the Import Substitution by Products Manufactured by Chinese Foreign Equity Joint Ventures and Chinese Foreign Cooperative Joint Ventures (1987), in *China Economic News*, Nov. 8, 1987, p. 7.

Agreement between the United States of America and People's Republic of China for the Avoidance of Double Taxation and Prevention of Tax Evasion with Respect to Income Taxes (1987), in CCH *Tax Treaties*, vol. 1, para. 1447.

Notice of the Beijing Tax Bureau on Reduction of Individual Income Tax (1987) (author's copy).

Implementing Rules for Examination and Confirmation of Export Enterprises and Technologically Advanced Enterprises With Foreign Investment (1987), in *China Economic News*, Nov. 7, 1987, p. 9.

Provisional Regulations of the Ministry of Finance on the Imposition of ICCT and Foreign Enterprise Tax on Foreign Representative Offices ("Zhonghua renmin gongheguo caizhengbu dui waiguo qiye changzhu daibiao jigou zhengshou gongshang tongyi shui, qiye suode shui de zanxing guiding") (1985), in Li Bichang, ed., *Zhongguo dui wai shui shou falu zhidu* (China's legal system for taxation of foreigners) (Beijing: Law Publishers, 1988), p. 279.

Administrative Provisions on the Calculation and Settling of Prices in Foreign Currency within China by Enterprises with Foreign Investment (1989), in CCH, para. 8–730.

State Council Measures for the Encouragement of Foreign Investment (1989), in CCH, para. 13–509.

Notice Concerning Questions of the Imposition of ICCT to Joint Ventures, Cooperative Production and Cooperative Managed Enterprises, and Independent Enterprises

("Guanyu dui wai heze jingying qiye, hezuo shengchan hezuo jingying qiye he ge shang duli jingying qiye zhengshou gongshang tongyi shui wenti de tongzhi"), in State Taxation Bureau, *Shui fa da chuan* (Encyclopedia of tax law) (Beijing: Finance and Economy Publishers, 1989), p. 524.

Regulations on Industrial and Commercial Consolidated Tax (1958) ("Zhonghua renmin gongheguo gong shang tong yi shui tiaoli"), in State Taxation Bureau, *Zhongguo she wai shuishoufagui ji* (Volume of PRC laws and regulations on foreign taxation) (Beijing: Finance and Tax Publishers, 1989), p. 217.

Detailed Rules for the Implementation of the Regulations on Industrial and Commercial Consolidated Tax (1958) ("Zhonghua renmin gongheguo gong shang tong yi shui tiaoli shixing xize"), in State Taxation Bureau, *Zhongguo she wai shuishou fagui ji* (Volume of PRC laws and regulations on foreign taxation) (Beijing: Finance and Tax Publishers, 1989), p. 228.

Income Tax Law of the People's Republic of China for Enterprises with Foreign Investment and Foreign Enterprises (1991), CCH, para. 32–505.

Implementing Rules for the Income Tax Law of the People's Republic of China for Enterprises with Foreign Investment and Foreign Enterprises (1991), in CCH, para. 32–507.

Law of the PRC on Administration of Taxation (1992), in CCH, para. 30–545.

PRC, Administration of the Finances of Foreign Investment Enterprises Provisions (1992), in *China Law and Practice*, Oct. 1, 1992, p. 22.

Supplement to Implementory Rules of MOFERT for Examination and Confirmation of Export Enterprises and Technologically Advanced Enterprises with Foreign Investment (1992), in *China Economic News*, Nov. 19, 1992, p. 7.

Individual Income Tax Law of the People's Republic of China (1993), in CCH, para. 30–500.

Announcement of the People's Bank of China on Further Reforming the Foreign Exchange Management System (1993), in CCH, para. 8–716.

Decision on the Use of Interim Regulations Concerning Value-Added Taxes, Consumption Taxes and Business Taxes on FFEs and Foreign Enterprises (1993), in *China Economic News*, Jan. 31, 1994, p. 7.

Implementing Regulations for the Individual Income Tax Law of the People's Republic of China (1994), in CCH, para. 30–305.

Provisional Regulations of the PRC on Value-Added Tax (1994), in *China Economic News*, Jan. 3, 1994, p. 9.

Value Added Tax Implementing Rules (1994), in "Special Supplement on Taxation," in *China Economic News*, Supplement no. 1, Jan. 31, 1994, p. 2.

Provisional Regulations of the PRC on Consumption Taxes (1994), in *China Economic News*, Jan. 17, 1994, p. 7.

Consumption Tax Implementing Regulations (1994), in "Special Supplement on Taxation," in *China Economic News*, Supplement no. 1, Jan. 31, 1994, p. 6.

Provisional Regulations of the PRC on Business Taxes (1994), in *China Economic News*, Jan. 17, 1994, p. 10.

Business Tax Implementing Regulations (1994), in "Special Supplement on Taxation," in *China Economic News*, Supplement no. 1, Jan. 31, 1994, p. 9.

Provisional Regulations of the PRC on Land Value-Added Taxes (1994), in *China Economic News*, Jan. 17, 1994, p. 7.

Chapter 6. Dispute Resolution

Convention on the Recognition and Enforcement of Foreign Arbitral Awards, in TIAS 6997, 330 UNTS 3 (1958).

UN Convention on Service Abroad of Judicial and Extrajudicial Documents in Civil or Commercial Matters, in TIAS 6638, 658 UNTS 163 (1965).

UN Convention on Collection of Evidence Abroad, in TIAS 7444, 847 UNTS 231 (1970).

Agreement on Trade Relations Between the U.S.A. and P.R.C. (1979), in 31 U.S.T. 4651.

Ministry of Justice Report to the National Conference on Judicial Administrative Work (1980) ("Sifabu guanyu quan guo sifa xingzheng gongzuo tanhui de baogao"), in *Zhonghua renmin gongheguo guowuyuan gongbao* (PRC State Council Bulletin) (1980), pp. 639, 641.

Organic Law of the People's Courts of the People's Republic of China (1979), in Yu Manking, ed., *A Full Translation of the Criminal Law Code and 3 Other Codes of the PRC* (Hong Kong: Great Earth Book Co., 1980), p. 111.

Civil Procedure Law of the People's Republic of China (Trial Implementation) (1982), in *Selections From World Broadcasts*, Mar. 17, 1982, p. C/1.

Constitution of the People's Republic of China (1982), in CCH, para. 4–500.

Provisional Rules of Procedure of the Foreign Trade Arbitration Commission (1956), in Owen Nee, ed., *Commercial Business and Trade Laws, People's Republic of China*, Booklet no. 15, Nov. 1983, p. L.3.

Regulations on Arbitration for Economic Contracts of the People's Republic of China (1983), in CCH, para. 10–620.

Foreign Economic Contract Law of the PRC (1985), in CCH, para. 5–550.

Notice Concerning the Enforcement of United Nations Convention on the Recognition and Enforcement of Foreign Arbitral Awards Acceded to by Our Country, PRC Supreme People's Court Circular No. 5, April 10, 1987 (author's copy).

Arbitration Rules of the China Maritime Arbitration Commission (1988), in CCH, para. 10–545.

Arbitration Provisions of the China International Economic and Trade Arbitration Commission (1989), in CCH, para. 10–505.

Civil Procedure Law of the People's Republic of China (1991), in CCH, para. 19–200.

1994 CIETAC amended arbitral rules discussed in Chen Dejun, "Report on the Amendment Draft of the Arbitration Rules of China International Economic and Trade Arbitration Commission" (unpublished), cited in Zhang Yulin, "Towards The UNCITRAL Model Law: A Chinese Perspective," in *Journal of International Arbitration*, vol. 11, no. 1, Mar. 1994, p. 87. Text of rules appear in Starkey B. Lubman and Gregory C. Wajnowski, "International Commercial Dispute Resolution in China: A Practical Assessment," in *The American Review of International Arbitration*, vol. 4, no. 2, 1993, p. 107.

Legal and Economic Reform, 1978–1993
A Partial Chronology

I. The Initial Opening: 1978–1980

1978

February: National Science Conference, at which intellectuals described as mental workers, considered members of working classes.

April: Eleventh Central Committee of CPC and Fifth National People's Congress issue "Decision on Certain Questions of Accelerating Industrial Development," setting the stage for reform of industrial production.

June: National Military Work Conference, Deng advocates "seeking truth from facts."

November–December: Third Plenum of the Eleventh Central Committee of the CPC: Announcement of "Open Door Policy"; Commencement of economic reform in agriculture; Commencement of legal reform.

1979

January: Announcement of one-child-per-family policy.

July: Second Session of Fifth National People's Congress: Enactment of Joint Venture Law and six other draft laws.

October: National People's Congress endorses return to private plots in agriculture.

---

*This chronology is necessarily partial, but I have tried to mention the salient developments in legal and economic reform as they related to China's foreign economic relations. *Sources*: Roderick MacFarquhar, ed., *The Politics of China 1949–1989* (Cambridge: Cambridge University Press, 1993); Pitman B. Potter, *The Economic Contract Law of China: Legitimation and Contract Autonomy in the PRC* (Seattle and London: University of Washington Press, 1992); Deborah Davis and Ezra Vogel, eds., *Chinese Society on the Eve of Reform* (Cambridge, MA.: Council on East Asian Studies/Harvard University, 1990); Samuel P. S. Ho and Ralph Huenemann, *China's Open Door Policy: The Quest for Foreign Technology & Capital* (Vancouver: UBC Press, 1984); CCH Australia, Ltd., *China Laws for Foreign Business*; *China Law and Practice*; *China Economic News*; *Zhonghua renmin gonghegro gongye qiye fa gui xuanbian* (Compilation of laws and regulations of the PRC on industrial enterprises) (Beijing: Law Publishers, 1981).

1980

March: Foreign exchange certificates issued (no public regulations as yet).

June: Provisional regulations issued for import and export licensing system.

July: Third Session of Fifth National People's Congress: Enactment of Joint Venture Income Tax Law; enactment of regulations on registration of joint ventures; enactment of joint venture labor regulations; enactment of regulations on Special Economic Zones (Fifteenth Session of Fifth NPC Standing Committee).

October: State Council approves regulations on registration of foreign representative offices.

December: State Council issues "Provisional Regulations on Exchange Control," in force, March 1, 1981.

II. Consolidation of Reforms: 1981–1985

1981

August: Regulations issued governing foreign exchange for foreign government institutions in China.

November: Guangdong People's Congress issues regulations on Shenzhen special economic zone.

November–December: Fourth Session of Fifth National People's Congress: Enactment of Economic Contract Law of the PRC; enactment of Foreign Enterprise Income Tax Law. By year end, 73 percent of rural households are using contracting system and 80 percent of industries are using profit retention system.

1982

January: CPC Document No. 1 supports expansion of new contracting system; foreign exchange control regulations governing individuals promulgated; regulations issued on offshore petroleum exploration; regulations issued on export licensing.

February: Implementing Regulations for Foreign Enterprise Income Tax Law issued.

March: Civil Procedure Law of the PRC issued.

April: Enactment of new Constitution, with specific provisions supporting foreign investment enterprises.

May: State Council establishes Commission on Reform of the Economic System.

August: Trademark law issued.

September: Twelfth National CPC Congress reaffirms Deng Xiaoping reform program.

December: Fifth Session of Fifth NPC ratifies Constitution.

1983

January: CPC Document No. 1 endorses rural decollectivization.

February: Bank of China issues regulations on establishment of foreign bank representative offices.

March: State Council issues implementing regulations for Trademark Law.

April: Policy of replacing taxes with profit (*li gai shui*) adopted for state industrial enterprises.

June: Sixth National People's Congress—Premier Zhao Ziyang announces retrenchment policy.

August: Foreign exchange controls for foreign businesses go into effect; regulations on arbitration of domestic contracts issued.

September: Second Session of Sixth National People's Congress: Sanctions announced for "economic crimes"; Implementing Regulations for the Joint Venture Law issued.

October: Second Plenum of Twelfth CPC Central Committee launches attack on "spiritual pollution."

1984

January: CPC Document No. 1 expands rural reforms: land contracting, broader autonomy in labor and capital circulation. State Council issues regulations on import licensing system. State Council issues regulations for commodity inspection system.

February: Guangdong Provincial Government enacts foreign economic contract law and technology import provisions for Shenzhen SEZ.

March: Fourth Session of Sixth National People's Congress Standing Committee enacts Patent Law.

May: Factory manager responsibility system begun; import licensing rules issued.

June: Implementing regulations issued for commodity inspection.

October: Third Plenum of Twelfth CPC Central Committee endorses "commodity economy," attacks "iron rice bowl."

November: National People's Congress endorses "one country two systems" for Hong Kong. State Council issues regulations for reduction of and elimination of enterprise income tax and industrial commercial consolidated tax in SEZ and 14 Coastal Cities.

1985

January: CPC Document No. 1 calls for further decollectivization and privatization of agriculture. State Council approves Patent Law Implementing Regulations.

March: Foreign Economic Contract Law enacted by Tenth Session of Sixth Standing Committee; State Council issues regulations on import and export tariffs. Ministry of Finance issues regulations for accounting in joint ventures. Ministry of Foreign Economic Relations and Trade issues new rules on export licensing system.

April: CPC Central Committee calls for further wage and price reform.

May: State Council approves regulations on contracts for importation of technology.

III. Acceleration of Reforms: 1986–1989

1986

January: State Council issues provisional regulations on foreign exchange balancing for joint ventures. National People's Congress endorses General Principles of Civil Law (to go into effect 1987).

April: Wholly Foreign-Owned Enterprise Law enacted.

July: China applies to restore its status as a signatory to the GATT.

August: National People's Congress endorses Bankruptcy Law.

October: State Council issues "Provisions on Encouragement of Foreign Investment" (22 Articles). Implementing regulations issued December 1986–April 1987.

December: Student demonstrations in Shanghai, Beijing, and other cities.

1987

January: Enlarged meeting of Central Committee-Politburo. Hu Yaobang dismissed. Campaign against "bourgeois liberalization." Customs Law enacted by Nineteenth Session of Sixth National People's Congress Standing Committee. China joins New York Convention on Recognition and Enforcement of Foreign Arbitral Awards.

April: China's accession to New York Convention on Recognition and Enforcement of Foreign Arbitral Awards becomes effective. Supreme People's Court issues notice on compliance with New York Convention.

October: Thirteenth CPC National Congress endorses further reforms—"China in early stages of socialism." Reform-oriented Politburo Standing Committee named.

December: State Council approves implementing rules for regulations on contracts for importation of technology. State Council approves regulations aimed at controlling contributions of capital to joint ventures.

1988

January: State Council approves Trademark Law Implementing Regulations. Supplemental regulations issued on corruption and bribery.

March: Second Plenum of Thirteenth CPC Central Committee reiterates call for commodity economy.

April: Seventh National People's Congress: Bankruptcy Law adopted; expansion of private businesses approved; Constitution amended to permit transfer of land use rights; State-Owned Enterprise Law adopted; Cooperative Joint Venture Law adopted; quality licensing system for imports initiated.

June: State Council enacts regulations on encouraging investment by Taiwan compatriots; State Council issues Stamp Tax regulations.

August: Financial crisis leads to runs on state banks.

September: Third Plenum of Thirteenth CPC Central Committee adopts retrenchment policies. China Council for the Promotion of International Trade issues "Arbitration Provisions for the China International Economic and Trade Arbitration Commission."

October: State Council and Fourth Session of Seventh National People's Congress reaffirm retrenchment policies. Curtails price reforms. Maintains "two-track" pricing system.

IV. Political Crisis and Rekindling of Reforms

1989

April–June: Political crisis leads to dismissal of Zhao Ziyang and Tiananmen massacre.

April: Administrative Litigation Law enacted.

May: China concludes Memorandum of Understanding with the United States on improving intellectual property protection.

December: Environmental Protection Law enacted.

1990

April: Third Session of Seventh National People's Congress approves revisions to Joint Venture Law, inter alia permitting foreign nationals to serve as Board of Directors Chair and removing limitations on duration.

May: State Council promulgates "Interim Regulations Concerning Administration of Investing, Developing, and Managing Sizable Land by Foreign Investors."

September: Copyright Law enacted by Fifteenth Session of Seventh National People's Congress Standing Committee.

October: State Council approves Implementing Regulations for Law on Wholly Foreign-Owned Enterprises.

December: Securities exchanges officially opened in Shanghai and Shenzhen.

1991

April: National People's Congress issues unified foreign enterprise tax law, harmonizing the tax treatment of foreign enterprises and foreign investment enterprises.

May: State Council issues regulations on computer software protection. Guangdong Provincial Government issues regulations on permitting foreign participation in land rights in the SEZs.

June: Copyright Law Implementing Regulations issued. People's Bank of China issues new regulations expanding scope of activities for foreign bank representative offices.

September: China accedes to International Convention on Contracts for the Sale of Goods.

November: Shanghai issues regulations permitting foreign investment in B Shares at Shanghai Securities Exchange.

1992

January: Deng Xiaoping tours Southern China. Deng speech calling for faster economic growth circulated to senior cadres as Internal Document No. 2 of 1992. China concludes second memorandum of understanding with the United States on intellectual property protection. Shenzhen issues regulations permitting foreign investment in B Shares on Shenzhen securities exchange.

March: State Council issues regulations imposing stricter rules for confirmation of export-oriented and advanced technology enterprises (first recognized under "22 Articles"). National People's Congress adopts Li Peng's call for slower growth despite criticism from some members.

June: Ministry of Finance issues new regulations on administration of finances in foreign investment enterprises.

July: Fourteenth National CPC Congress adopts concept of "socialist market economy" to replace "socialist commodity economy," indicating effort to extend market policies to noncommodity sectors (services, energy, finance). Supreme People's Court issues "Opinion on Several Questions Concerning the Application of the Civil Procedure Law of the PRC," clarifying the handling of civil cases involving foreign parties.

September: State Council issues provisions on compliance with international copyright treaties.

October: China joins Berne Convention for the Protection of Literary and Artistic Works. China concludes market access agreement with the United States.

November: State Council issues regulations permitting foreign investment in retailing operations in China.

December: Economic growth hits 12.1% (as compared to 7 percent in 1991; 5.2 percent in 1990; and 4 percent in 1989). Party General Secretary Jiang Zemin addresses national economic planning conference, calls for measures to prevent economy from "overheating."

1993

February: Trademark Law amended to permit registration of service marks and to simplify procedures for registration of trademarks in multiple categories.

March: PRC Constitution amended to entrench emphasis on market economy and diminish role of state planning.

April: National People's Congress gives formal approval to Three Gorges Dam construction project.

September: Economic Contract Law amended, inter alia to remove references to sanctity of state plan.

October: State Council issues regulations on cooperation in development of onshore petroleum.

December: People's Bank of China decision to eliminate Foreign Exchange Certificates and reform foreign exchange system. Fifth Session of Eighth National People's Congress Standing Committee approves State Council regulations on application of value-added tax, consumption tax, and business tax to foreign enterprises and foreign investment enterprises, and annulment of the Industrial-Commercial Consolidated Tax.

Partial List of Interview Subjects

Representative of a major foreign law firm in Beijing.

Representative of U.S. trading organization in Beijing.

Representative of major U.S. corporation resident in Beijing.

Official of the foreign government commerce office, Shanghai.

Beijing-based representative of foreign owned enterprise, who works closely with major U.S. Corporations.

Representatives from national legal research facility, Beijing.

Representatives of Policy Institute of the State Planning Commission.

Representatives from Treaty and Law Department, Ministry of Foreign Trade and Economic Cooperation, Beijing.

Scholars from Shanghai legal research facility.

The author would like to indicate that the opinions and recommendations expressed in this book do not necessarily reflect those of any particular individual(s) interviewed during the course of research on this project.

Notes

The following abbreviations have been used in these notes:

Alb. L. Rev.	*Albany Law Review*
Am. J. Comp. L.	*American Journal of Comparative Law*
Cal. L. Rev.	*California Law Review*
Can. Bus. L. J.	*Canadian Business Law Journal*
China L. Rep.	*China Law Reporter*
Columbia J. of Transnational L.	*Columbia Journal of Transnational Law*
I. L. M.	*International Legal Materials*
Int'l & Comp. L. Q.	*International and Comparative Law Quarterly*
Int'l J. of Psychology	*International Journal of Psychology*
Int'l Lawyer	*The International Lawyer*
J. Chinese L.	*Journal of Chinese Law*
J. of Int'l Arb.	*Journal of International Arbitration*
Law. and Soc. Rev.	*Law and Society Review*
NCNA	*New China News Agency*
S. Calif. L. Rev.	*Southern California Law Review*
Stanford J. Int'l L.	*Stanford Journal of International Law*
Texas Int'l L. J.	*Texas International Law Journal*
UCLA Pac. Basin L. J.	*UCLA Pacific Basin Law Journal*
U. Pitt. L. Rev.	*University of Pittsburgh Law Review*
Wisc. L. Rev.	*Wisconsin Law Review*
Yale L. J.	*Yale Law Journal*

Chapter 1

1. Although Weber recognized that law affects other aspects of society as well, he was quite clear on the interplay between formal legal rationality and economic activity in Europe. See Max Weber, *Economy and Society* (Roth and Wittich, eds.) (Berkeley and Los Angeles: University of California Press, 1978), pp. 333–37, wherein Weber states on p. 334, "Obviously, legal guarantees are directly at the service of economic interests to a very large extent . . . economic interests are among the strongest factors influencing the creation of law." It must be conceded, though, that less critical readers of Weber bear responsibility for expanding his theories beyond the subtle confines to which he subjected them. For a discussion of this problem, see generally,

David Trubek, "Toward a Social Theory of Law: An Essay on the Study of Law and Politics in Economic Development," in 82 *Yale L. J.* 1 (1972), and "Max Weber on Law and the Rise of Capitalism," in *Wisc. L. Rev.* 3 (1972), p. 722.

2. Prominent in this effort was the work of a group of Yale University legal scholars, of whom perhaps Professor David Trubek is best known. See, for example, "Toward a Social Theory of Law: An Essay on the Study of Law and Development," 82 *Yale L. J.* 1 (1972). Alan Watson's work on legal transplanting was an important component of this approach. See Alan Watson, *Legal Transplants: An Approach to Comparative Law* (Charlottesburg, VA: University Press of Virginia, 1974). Professor Trubek's views have evolved significantly over the years, and he now focuses on what he terms the political economy of legal change. See David M. Trubek, Yves Dezalay, Ruth Buchanan, and John R. Davis, "Global Restructuring and the Law: The Internationalization of Legal Fields and the Creation of Transnational Areas," (Global Studies Research Program Working Paper Series on the Political Economy of Legal Change, University of Wisconsin-Madison, 1993), esp. pp. 50, et seq., where the authors address the relationship between legal reform and competition for investment, and conclude by calling for a new approach that inter alia links legal to economic and political fields.

3. For a discussion of the problems faced by efforts to transplant American law to Latin America, see James A. Gardner, *Legal Imperialism: American Lawyers and Foreign Aid in Latin America* (Madison: University of Wisconsin Press, 1980).

4. See generally, Franz Schurmann, *The Logic of World Power* (New York: Pantheon, 1974), esp. chapters 1 and 2.

5. See generally, Richard Barnet, *The Lean Years: Politics in the Age of Scarcity* (New York: Touchstone, 1980); Wil Hout, *Capitalism and the Third World* (Aldershot: E. Elgar, 1993).

6. See generally, Stephen P. Riley, *The Politics of Global Debt* (New York: St. Martin's Press, 1993); Gianni Vaggi, ed., *From the Debt Crisis to Sustainable Development: Changing Perspectives on North-South Development* (1993).

7. See, for example, Daniel S. Lev "Judicial Authority and the Struggle For an Indonesian Rechstaat," 13 *Law and Soc. Rev.* 37 (1978).

8. See, for example, Francis G. Snyder, "Law and Development in the Light of Dependency Theory," 14 *Law and Soc. Rev.* 722 (1980). Also see James A. Gardner, *Legal Imperialism.*

9. See, for example, G. Sidney Silliman, "Dispute Processing by the Philippine Agrarian Court," 16 *Law and Soc. Rev.* 89 (1981) and J. Joseph Burns, "Civil Courts and the Development of Commercial Relations: The Case of North Sumatra," 15 *Law and Soc. Rev.* 347 (1980).

10. See generally, Harold J. Berman, *Law and Revolution: The Formation of the Western Legal Tradition* (Cambridge, MA: Harvard University Press, 1983); Michael Tigar and Marion Levy, *Law and the Rise of Capitalism* (New York: The Free Press, 1977).

11. Although certainly there has been debate within the Chinese leadership on virtually all aspects of economic and legal reform, there has emerged a broad consensus view that the two are interlinked. For but a few examples, see generally "Zhongguo gongchandang di shi yi jie zhongyang weiyuanhui di san ci quanti huiyi gongbao" (Communique of the Third Plenum of the Eleventh CCP Central Committee), in *Hongqi*

(Red Flag), 1979, no. 1, pp. 14–21, at p. 19. Also see Peng Zhen, "Explanation on the Seven Draft Laws Made at the Second Session of the Fifth NPC on 26th June, 1979," *NCNA*, in *Selections From World Broadcasts*, July 4, 1979, p. FE/6158/C/1. Also see James V. Feinerman, "Economic and Legal Reform in China 1978–91," in *Problems of Communism*, Sept.–Oct., 1991, p. 62; and Yin Liangpei, ed., *Jingji gaige yu jingji fazhi* (Economic reform and the economic legal system) (Shenyang: Liaoning University Press, 1985).

12. See, for example, Ssu-fa Hsing-cheng pu (Department of Justice and Administration), *T'ai-wan Min-shih Hsi-kuan Tiao-ch'a Pao-kao* (Report on Investigation of Civil Customs in Taiwan) (Taipei: 1968). Also see Donald DeClopper, "Doing Business in Lukang," in Arthur Wolf, ed., *Studies in Chinese Society* (Stanford, 1978) and Michael J. Moser, *Law and Social Change in a Chinese Community: A Case Study from Rural Taiwan* (Dobbs Ferry, NY: Oceana, 1982).

13. See, for example, Hui-chen Wang Liu, *The Traditional Chinese Clan Rules* (New York: J. J. Augustin, 1959); Susan Greenhalgh, "Families and Networks in Taiwan's Economic Development," in Edwin A. Winckler and Susan Greenhalgh, eds., *Contending Approaches to the Political Economy of Taiwan* (Armonk, NY and London: M. E. Sharpe, 1988, p. 224); Hwang Kwang-kuo, "Modernization of the Chinese Family Business," in 123 *Int'l J. of Psychology* 593 (1990); and Thomas B. Gold, "Urban Private Business and Social Change," in Deborah Davis and Ezra F. Vogel, eds., *Chinese Society on the Eve of Tiananmen: The Impact of Reform* (Cambridge, MA and London: Council on East Asian Studies/Harvard University, 1990). For discussion of the extent to which formal law remained influential in traditional China, see Hugh Scogin, "Between Heaven and Man: Contract and the State in Han Dynasty China," in 63 *S. Calif. L. Rev.* 1325 (1990).

14. See, for example, Stanley B. Lubman, "Mao and Mediation: Politics and Dispute Resolution in Communist China", in 55 *Cal. L. Rev.* 1284 (1967). Also see Pitman B. Potter, *Legitimacy and Contract Autonomy in the People's Republic of China: The Economic Contract Law of China* (Seattle and London: University of Washington Press, 1992).

15. For an overview of economic reform policies after 1978, see, for example, Harry Harding, *China's Second Revolution: Reform After Mao* (Washington, D.C.: The Brookings Institution, 1987); Elizabeth Perry and Christine Wong, eds., *The Political Economy of Reform in Post-Mao China* (Cambridge, MA: Harvard University Press, 1985).

16. For an overview, see James V. Feinerman, "Economic and Legal Reform in China, 1978–91," in *Problems of Communism*, Sept.-Oct., 1991, p. 62.

17. See Pitman B. Potter, "Riding the Tiger: Legitimacy and Legal Culture in Post-Mao China," in *The China Quarterly* 138 (June, 1994). p. 325.

18. For discussion of China's trade reforms see, for example, Nicholas R. Lardy, *Foreign Trade and Economic Reform in China: 1978–1990* (Cambridge: Cambridge University Press, 1992). For discussion of investment issues, see Robert Kleinberg, *China's "Opening" to the Outside World: The Experiment with Foreign Capitalism* (Boulder, CO: Westview, 1990). A chronology of selected developments in China's economic and legal reforms is included in Appendix B.

19. See Hong Kong Trade Development Council Research Department, *China's Foreign Trade System* (May, 1991).

20. See generally, Margaret M. Pearson, *Joint Ventures in the People's Republic of China* (Princeton: Princeton University Press, 1991), pp. 135 et seq.

21. See generally, Jerome A. Cohen and Stuart J. Valentine, "China Business—Problems and Prospects," in William P. Streng and Allen D. Wilcox, eds., *Doing Business in China* (New York: Matthew Bender, 1992), p. I-1.

22. James V. Feinerman, "Chinese Law Relating to Foreign Investment and Trade: The Decade of Reform in Retrospect," in Joint Economic Committee of U.S. Congress, *China's Economic Dilemmas in the 1990s: The Problems of Reforms, Modernization, and Interdependence* (Washington, D.C.: U.S. Government Printing Office, 1991), p. 828.

23. Robert G. Sutter, "External Factors Affecting the Economy," in Joint Economic Committee of U.S. Congress, *China's Economic Dilemmas in the 1990s: The Problems of Reforms, Modernization, and Interdependence*, p. 48.

24. Chinese language sources for PRC legal materials include *Zhonghua renmin gongheguo xianxing fagui huibian* (Compilation of current laws and regulations of the PRC) (Beijing: Law Publishers, yearly); *Zhongguo jingji tequ kaifaqu falu fagui xuanbian* (Compilation of laws and regulations for China's special economic zones and open areas) (Beijing: 1987); Ministry of Finance: Tax Bureau and Treaties and Law Division, *Shewai shuiwu zhishi* (Knowledge on foreign taxation) (Beijing: 1987); State Taxation Bureau, *Zhongguo shewai shuishou fa gui ji* (Collection of income tax laws and regulations of China) (Beijing: 1990); *Renmin ribao* (People's Daily); *Fazhi ribao* (Legal System Daily); and *Guoji shang bao* (Journal of International Commerce).

    English-language sources include *Laws for Foreign Business* (CCH Australia Ltd.); *China's Foreign Economic Legislation Vol. I–III* (Beijing: Foreign Languages Press, 1982, 1986, 1987); Dept. of Treaties and Law, Ministry of Foreign Economic Relations and Trade, *Collection of Laws and Regulations of the People's Republic of China Concerning Foreign Economic Affairs* (Beijing: Law Publishers, periodical); Victor Nee, ed., *Commercial Business and Trade Laws, People's Republic of China*, (Dobbs Ferry, NY: Oceana, looseleaf); *China Economic News*; *China Law and Practice*; Yu Manking, ed., *A Full Translation of the Criminal Law Code and 3 Other Codes of the PRC* (Hong Kong: Great Earth Book Co., 1980); *The China Business Review* and *East Asian Executive Reports*.

    A list of legal and regulatory materials cited is given in Appendix A. Unless otherwise indicated, all citations are to CCH Australia, *China Laws for Foreign Business* (looseleaf), as follows: CCH, para. no. ———.

25. For a partial listing of interview subjects, see Appendix C. These subjects add to the multitude of clients and colleagues with whom discussion on issues of law and foreign business in China has taken place since 1985.

26. See, for example, Stanley B. Lubman, "Studying Contemporary Chinese Law: Limits, Possibilities and Strategy," in 34 *Am. J. Comp. L.* 293 (1991); and Yu Xingzhong, "Legal Pragmatism in the People's Republic of China," in 3 *J. Chinese Law* 29 (1989). Also see generally, Ronald C. Keith, *China's Struggle for the Rule of Law* (New York: St. Martin's Press, 1994), pp. 218–21.

27. See Derk Bodde and Clarence Morris, *Law in Imperial China* (Philadelphia: University of Pennsylvania Press, 1967); Michael Dutton, *Policing and Punishment in*

China: From Patriarchy to "The People" (Hong Kong: Oxford University Press, 1992).

28. See generally, Stanley B. Lubman, "Methodological Problems in Studying Chinese Communist 'Civil' Law," in Jerome A. Cohen, ed., *Contemporary Chinese Law: Research Problems and Perspectives* (Cambridge, MA: Harvard University Press, 1970).

29. See, for example, Victor H. Li, "The Evolution and Development of the Chinese Legal System," in John Lindbeck, *CHINA: Management of a Revolutionary Society* (Seattle and London: University of Washington Press, 1970), esp. pp. 240–41.

30. For example, see Peng Zhen, "Guanyu qi ge falu caoan de shuoming" (Explanation of seven draft laws), in Peng Zhen, *Lun xin shiqi de shehuizhu minzhu yu fazhi jianshe* (On the establishment of socialist democracy and legal system in the new period) (Beijing: Central Digest Publishers, 1989), p. 1.

31. For example, in October 1991, the Law Institute of the Chinese Academy of Social Sciences hosted an International Symposium on the Rule of Law in Social and Economic Development that addressed this issue specifically.

32. See List of Laws and Regulations, Appendix A. Specific examples of the instrumentalist orientation of laws and regulations governing China's foreign economic relations are discussed in the substantive chapters that follow.

33. In theory, the flexibility and discretion conferred on Chinese decisionmakers is controlled through ideological training in much the same way that the discretion of Imperial Chinese officials was controlled through Confucian training. See generally, Joseph Levenson, *Confucian China and Its Modern Fate* (Berkeley: University of California Press, 1958.)

34. See Appendix A.

35. See generally, James V. Feinerman, "Economic and Legal Reform in China, 1978–91"; and Stanley B. Lubman, "Emerging Functions of Formal Legal Institutions in China's Modernization," in Joint Economic Committee of U.S. Congress, ed., *China Under the Four Modernizations* (Washington, D.C.: U.S. Government Printing Office), p. 235. In another paper, I suggest an alternate approach to formalism in Chinese law, namely, one that interprets justice as compliance with formal rules regardless of substantive consequences. See Pitman B. Potter, "Riding the Tiger: Legitimacy and Legal Reform in Post-Mao China," in *The China Quarterly*, June 1994, p. 325. Also see Thomas C. Grey, "Langdell's Orthodoxy," in 45 *U. Pitt. L. Rev.* 1 (1983).

36. See, for example, Rui Mu, *Chinese Foreign Economic Law: Analysis and Commentary* (Washington, D.C.: International Law Institute, 1990).

37. See, for example, "China's Replies to Questions From GATT Contracting Parties Concerning the Memorandum on China's Foreign Trade System," *Intertrade*, Jan. 1988. Also see *Guanshui yu maoyi zong xieding yu Zhongguo* (GATT and China) (Beijing: 1992).

38. See "China Defends Copyright System Ahead of U.S. Sanction Threat," in Agence France Presse English Wire, June 16, 1994, reprinted in *China News Digest* (electronic media), June 16, 1994. Also see "White Paper on Intellectual Property Rights Published," in *FBIS Daily Report—China*, June 16, 1994, p. 32.

39. For a discussion of the problem of policy making and trade-offs, see Susan Shirk, *The Political Logic of Economic Reform in China* (Berkeley: University of Cal-

ifornia Press, 1993), in which the author uses the term "particularistic contracting" to describe a policy process by which consensus is reached through a series of agreements ("particularistic contracts") that confer on contending elite groups benefits sufficient to induce their support for the policy of the day. Also see Murray Scot Tanner, "Organizations and Politics in China's Post-Mao Law-Making System," in Pitman B. Potter, ed., *Domestic Law Reforms in Post-Mao China* (Armonk, NY and London: M. E. Sharpe, 1994), p. 56.

40. For an English-language text of the FECL with analysis, see Jerome Alan Cohen, "The New Foreign Contract Law," in *The China Business Review*, July-Aug. 1985.

41. An English-language text appears in Pitman B. Potter, *Legitimacy and Contract Autonomy in the PRC*. Also see Henry R. Zheng, "A Comparative Analysis of the Foreign Economic Contract Law of the People's Republic of China," in 4 *UCLA Pac. Basin L. J.* 30 (1985). For a brief review of selected aspects of the 1993 revisions to the ECL, see Pitman B. Potter, "Editor's Note," in *China Law and Practice*, Oct. 1993. The application of the ECL to contracts between joint ventures and Chinese units was specified in the "Decision of the Supreme People's Court of the PRC on Certain Questions Concerning the Implementation of the Foreign Economic Contract Law of the PRC" (Zuigao renmin fayuan guanyu shiyong shewai jingji hetong fa ruogan wenti de jueda), in Zhang Shouqiang, ed., *Hetong fa gui yu hetong shiyang huibian* (Compilation of Contract Laws and Regulations and Contract Forms) (Harbin: 1988), p. 960.

42. U.N. Doc. A/Conf. 97/18, reprinted in 19 *I.L.M.* 668 (1980).

43. For an English-language text with commentary see generally, William C. Jones, ed., *The General Principles of Civil Law of the People's Republic of China* (Armonk, NY: M. E. Sharpe, 1989).

44. See Constitution of the PRC (Beijing: Foreign Languages Press, 1982), Article 18. Also see 1993 constitutional amendments emphasizing the market economy in "Amendments to the PRC Constitution Adopted at the First Session of the Eighth National People's Congress on 29 March, 1993," in *FBIS Daily Report-China*, Mar. 30, 1993, p. 42.

45. See Pitman B. Potter, "China's New Land Development Regulations," *China Business Review*, March-April, 1991, p. 12.

46. See, for example, Ministry of Public Security Immigration Administration Bureau, *Zhonghua renmin gongheguo chu ru jing guanli fa gui huibian* (Compilation of laws and regulations on administration of emigration and immigration) (Beijing: 1987).

47. An English-language text of the ALL appears in Pitman B. Potter, "The Administrative Litigation Law of the PRC," in *China Law and Government*, Fall 1991.

48. ALL, Article 25.

49. ALL, Article 2.

50. ALL, Article 11.

51. See generally, Pitman B. Potter, "China's Administrative Litigation Law May Offer Some Protection Against Abuse of Power," *East Asian Executive Reports*, Nov. 15, 1990, p. 9.

52. This generally occurs as a result of requirements that applicants exhaust the process of administrative reconsideration (*fuyi*) before filing for judicial review. See generally, Pitman B. Potter, "The Administrative Litigation Law of the PRC," *Chinese Law and Government*, Fall 1991.

53. See generally, Michel Oksenberg, ed., *China's Participation in the IMF, the World Bank, and GATT: Toward a Global Economic Order* (Ann Arbor: University of Michigan Press, 1990); Susan MacCormac, "Eyeing the GATT," *The China Business Review* March-April, 1993, p. 34.
54. See "People's Republic of China-United States Memorandum of Understanding Concerning Market Access," 31 *I.L.M.* 1274 (1992).
55. The 1989 Memorandum of Agreement (MOU) is discussed in Pitman B. Potter, "Bettering Protection For Intellectual Property," 16 *China Business Review* 27 (1989). Also see Memorandum of Understanding Between the Government of the People's Republic of China and the Government of the United States of America on the Protection of Intellectual Property (1992).
56. See, for example, "EC Ambassador on Sino-European Trade," in *China Economic News*, June 28, 1993, p. 8.
57. See generally, John Wong, *Understanding China's Socialist Market Economy* (Singapore Times Academic Press, 1993), pp. 91, et seq.; Gary Hamilton, ed., *Business Networks and Economic Development in East and Southeast Asia* (Hong Kong: Centre of Asian Studies, University of Hong Kong, 1991), p. 3. Increased business ties between China and Taiwan are exemplified by the "Law of the PRC on the Protection of Taiwan Compatriots' Investment," enacted in 1994 based on earlier regulations. See *China Economic News*, Mar. 21, 1994, p. 6.

Chapter 2

1. See "Foreign Trade Law of the PRC" (1994), in *China Economic News*, May 23, 1994, p. 8, May 30, 1994, p. 7.
2. See generally, World Bank, *China: Foreign Trade Reform* (Washington, D.C.: The World Bank, 1994). Also see Hang-Sheng Cheng, "China's Foreign Trade Reform, 1979–91," 1990 Institute Phase I Issue Paper (Draft 1991).
3. See generally, Jamie Horsley, "The Regulation of China's Foreign Trade," in Michael J. Moser, ed., *Foreign Trade, Investment and the Law in the People's Republic of China*, 2d ed., (Hong Kong: Oxford University Press, 1987).
4. See generally, Jamie P. Horsley, "The Regulation of China's Foreign Trade."
5. Hong Kong Trade Development Council, *China's Foreign Trade System* (1991).
6. See, for example, the listing of "branches" of the China National Native Produce and Animal By-Products Import and Export Corporation, in Sun Yuzong, ed., *Dui wai jingji maoyi gongzuo shouce* (Handbook on Foreign Economic and Trade Work) (Beijing: Economic and Trade Publishers, 1988), pp. 835–49.
7. See Qiu Demin, *Zhongguo wai mao tizhi gaige gailun* (General theory on the reform of China's foreign trade system) (Xian: Shaanxi People's Press, 1988), pp. 100 et seq.
8. See *Dui wai maoyi qiye guanli* (Management of foreign trade) (Beijing: Foreign Trade Education Publishers, 1988), pp. 67–68.
9. See Hong Kong Trade Development Council, *China's Foreign Trade System.*
10. See Sun Zuojun, ed., *Dui wai maoyi kuaiji* (Accounting for foreign trade) (Shenyang: Liaoning People's Press, 1988), p. 204.
11. See, for example, "Interim Regulations on the Import Commodities Licensing System of the PRC" (1984), in CCH, para. 51–600; "Provisional Regulations Governing

the Export License System of the Administrative Commission on Import and Export and the Ministry of Foreign Trade" (1980), in CCH, para. 51–500.

12. See "State Council Regulations for the Encouragement of Foreign Investment" (1986), in CCH, para. 13–509, and "Ministry of Foreign Economic Relations and Trade Methods on the Purchase and Export of Domestic Products by Foreign Business Enterprises to Balance Income and Expenditures of Foreign Exchange" (1987), in CCII, para. 13–526; and "Measures Relating to the Import Substitution by Products Manufactured by Chinese-Foreign Equity Joint Ventures and Chinese-Foreign Cooperative Ventures" (1987), in CCH, para. 50–653.

13. See, for example, note 11, and accompanying text.

14. See, for example, "Details Concerning the Export License System Governing Eleven Categories of Export Commodities" (1982), in CCH, para. 51–520.

15. See Hong Kong Trade Development Council, *China's Foreign Trade System*.

16. See "Final Version of 14th CPC National Congress Report," in *FBIS Daily Report— China*, Oct. 21, 1992, pp. 1–21, at p. 8; and "Decision of the CPC Central Committee on Issues Concerning the Establishment of a Socialist Market Economic Structure" (Nov. 14, 1993), in *China Economic News*, 1993 Supplement No. 12, Nov. 29, 1993, pp. 6–9. In keeping with these changes, the revised text of the Economic Contract Law issued in 1993 deleted references to state planning and replaced them with references to state policies. See Economic Contract Law of the PRC (1993), in *China Law and Practice*.

17. See "Foreign Trade Law of the PRC."

18. "Regulations of the PRC on the Inspection of Imported and Exported Goods" (1984), in CCH, para. 16–600.

19. See, for example, "Implementing Regulations for the Quality License System for Imported Electrical and Mechanical Commodities (For Trial Use)" (1990), Article 3, in CCH, para. 51–620.

20. See "Customs Law of the PRC" (1987), in CCH, para. 50–300.

21. See "Foreign Trade Law of the PRC."

22. Heng-Sheng Cheng, "China's Foreign Trade Reform, 1979–91." Also see State Statistical Bureau, *Statistical Yearbook of China 1992*, as cited in John Wong, *Understanding China's Socialist Market Economy* (Singapore: Times Academic Press, 1993), pp. 66 and 71.

23. Ibid.

24. See "Statistical Communique of the State Statistical Bureau of the People's Republic of China on the 1993 National Economic and Social Development," in *China Economic News*, 1994 Supplement no. 3, Mar. 14, 1994, p. 5.

25. See, for example, Chen Chien-ping, "Why Did China Incur Trade Deficit Last Year?" in *Wen Wei Po* (HK), Feb. 3 and 4, 1993, reprinted in *FBIS Daily Report— China*, Feb. 9, 1994, pp. 32–34.

26. See generally, Kathleen Hartford, "The Political Economy Behind Beijing Spring," in Tony Saich, ed., *The Chinese People's Movement: Perspectives on Beijing Spring 1989* (Armonk, NY and London: M. E. Sharpe, 1990), p. 50.

27. See generally, Suzanne Ogden, *China's Unresolved Issues: Politics, Development, and Culture* (Englewood Cliffs, NJ: Prentice Hall, 1989), pp. 291, et seq. and pp. 294, et seq.

28. See generally, Kathleen Hartford, "The Political Economy Behind Beijing Spring."

29. Foreign Economic Contract Law of the PRC, Articles 4 and 9, wherein contracts are required to comply with the social and public interest of the PRC.
30. See Customs Law of the PRC, Article 1 ("[t]his law is formulated to safeguard China's . . . interests . . . "); Provisional Export Regulations, Preamble ("[t]he following articles are instituted for the purpose of intensifying the control of foreign trade"); and the Commodity Import Regulations, Article 1 ("[t]hese regulations are formulated with the purpose of strengthening the planned control of import trade . . . ").
31. FECL, Article 7.
32. See Trial Implementing Rules for the Quality License System in Imported Electromechanical Commodities, Article 1 ("These Implementing Rules are enacted in order to . . . safeguard the interests of the state . . . ").
33. The United States' dissatisfaction with the import inspection system was reflected in the 1992 Sino–U.S. market access agreement. See "People's Republic of China—United States Memorandum of Understanding Concerning Market Access."
34. See John Wong, *Understanding China's Socialist Economy* (Singapore: Times Academic Press, 1993), p. 73.
35. See, for example, Jiang Zemin, "Speed Up the Pace of Reform, Opening, and Modernization and Win Greater Victories in the Socialist Cause with Chinese Characteristics," Report to the Fourteenth CPC National Congress, Oct. 12, 1992, in *FBIS Daily Report—China: Supplement* Oct. 21, 1992, esp. pp. 12–13.
36. See, for example, "Seeking Progress Steadily To Join GATT," in *FBIS Daily Report*, Jul. 26, 1993, p. 42. Also see response to the Ministry of Foreign Economic Relations and Trade to certain questions concerning China's accession to the GATT (1987). Personal copy.
37. See generally, Robert Gilpin, "Three Models of the Future," in 29 *Int'l Organization* 37 (1975), extracted in Geore Modelski, *Transnational Corporations and World Order: Readings in International Political Economy* (San Francisco: W. H. Freeman and Co., 1979), pp. 353–72, at pp. 367–369. In the East Asian experience, state regulation of foreign trade has been aimed at pursuing a variety of development strategies, including import substitution, export led growth, and entrepôt growth. See Stephen Haggard, *Pathways From the Periphery: The Politics of Growth in the Newly Industrialized Countries* (Ithaca and London: Cornell University Press, 1990), Chapter 2. Regardless of the strategy pursued, however, it is the instrumentalist use of state regulation for national economic goals that is the hallmark of mercantilism.
38. See Robert Kleinberg, *China's "Opening" To the Outside World: The Experiment With Foreign Capitalism* (Boulder, San Francisco, and Oxford: Westview Press, 1990).
39. See, for example, Li Mei, "NAFTA and the Prospects for Sino–Canadian Trade Development," Beijing Central People's Radio (Mandarin) Dec. 1, 1993, tr. in *FBIS Daily Report—China* Dec. 3, 1992, p. 6; Wang Yong, "American Trade Bloc Could Hurt Competitors," *China Daily (Business Weekly Supplement)* Oct. 25, 1993, in *FBIS Daily Report—China* Oct. 27, 1993, p. 2. Also see Zhang Xinhua, "An Analysis of U.S. Economic and Trade Strategy Toward China."
40. This has been confirmed by numerous unstructured interviews conducted during 1992–93 in Beijing and Shanghai. For a partial listing, see Appendix C.
41. See "People's Republic of China—United States Memorandum of Understanding Concerning Market Access."

42. See "North American Free Trade Agreement" (Final Text), Dec. 17, 1992 (CCH International, 1992). For discussion, see "Annual Symposium: The North American Free Trade Agreement (NAFTA)," in 27 *Int'l Lawyer* 589 (1993).
43. See General Agreement in Tariffs and Trade (1947, as amended) TIAS 1700, 55 U.N.T.S. 187, IV GATT Basic Instrument and Selected Documents [BISD], Article XXIV. See generally, J. G. Castel, A. L. C. deMestral, and W. C. Graham, *International Business Transactions and Economic Relations* (Toronto: Emond Montgomery, 1986), pp. 73, 122.

Chapter 3

1. See "Joint Venture Law of the PRC" (1980, rev. 1990), in CCH, para. 6–500; "Implementing Regulations for the Joint Venture Law of the PRC" (1983, rev. 1986), in CCH, para. 6–550.
2. See Margaret M. Pearson, *Joint Ventures in the People's Republic of China* (Princeton: Princeton University Press, 1991), p. 80.
3. See Joint Venture Law, Article 4.
4. See Joint Venture Law Implementing Regulations, Article 32.
5. See Joint Venture Law Implementing Regulations, Articles 33 and 36.
6. See "National People's Congress Revision of the PRC Sino-Foreign Equity Joint Venture Law Decision," para. 3 (re: JV Law Article 6), in *China Law and Practice*, May 7, 1990, p. 36.
7. See Joint Venture Law Implementing Regulations, Articles 39 and 40.
8. Article 16 of the Joint Venture Law Implementing Regulations requires the parties to specify the management structure and procedures to be employed in the venture and detail other items to be included in the articles of association. Procedures on registration are set forth in the Joint Venture Law Implementing Regulations Articles 8–18, and in Procedures of the PRC for the Registration and Administration of Chinese-Foreign Joint Ventures ("Joint Venture Registration Procedures"), in *China's Foreign Economic Legislation Vol. I* (Beijing: Foreign Languages Press, 1982), pp. 13–16.
9. See Joint Venture Registration Procedures; Joint Venture Law Implementing Regulations, Articles 6 and 11.
10. See "Law of the People's Republic of China on Sino–Foreign Cooperative Enterprises" (1988) (Cooperative Enterprise Law), in CCH, para. 6–100.
11. See Cooperative Enterprise Law, Article 12.
12. See Joint Venture Registration Procedures.
13. See Cooperative Enterprise Law, Article 5.
14. See Cooperative Enterprise Law, Articles 2 and 6.
15. The first and perhaps most highly publicized case of a WFOE is the 3M operation in Shanghai set up in 1983.
16. See "Law on Enterprises Operated Exclusively With Foreign Capital" (hereafter "WFOE Law") (1986), in CCH, para. 13–506.
17. See WFOE Law, Article 5. Uncertainties remain, however, over the meaning of the terms "special circumstances" and "reasonable compensation"—particularly in light of China's support for policies associated with the "New International Economic Order" that favor strict controls over foreign investment and the primacy of host-state sovereignty. See generally, "Charter of Economic Rights and Duties of States"

(UN GA Resolution 3281 (XXIX), Dec. 12, 1974); Samuel Asante, "International Law and Foreign Investment: A Reappraisal," in 37 *Int't & Comp. L. Q.* 588 (1988); Jercy Makarczyk, *Principles of a New International Economic Order* (Dordrecht: M. Nijhoff, 1988).

18. See Richard Pomfret, *Investing in China* (Ames, IA: Iowa University Press, 1991), p. 65.

19. See "Implementing Rules for the Law of the PRC on Wholly Foreign-Owned Enterprises" (1990), in CCH, para. 13–507.

20. See WFOE Implementing Regulations, Article 4.

21. See WFOE Implementing Regulations, Article 5.

22. See "Regulations of the People's Republic of China on the Exploitation of Offshore Petroleum Resources in Cooperation with Foreign Enterprises" (1982), in CCH, para. 14–560. Also see Michael J. Moser, "Legal Aspects of Offshore Oil and Gas Exploration and Development in China," in Michael J. Moser, ed., *Foreign Trade, Investment, and the Law in the People's Republic of China* (2d ed.) (Hong Kong: Oxford University Press, 1987), p. 270.

23. See "Regulations of the PRC on Sino–Foreign Cooperation in the Development of Continental Petroleum Resources" (1993), in *China Economic News*, Nov. 15, 1993, p. 7. For discussion of new regulations on foreign-invested mining operations, see China Daily, Feb. 21, 1994.

24. See "Interim Regulations Concerning the Control of Resident Offices of Foreign Enterprises," in CCH, para. 7–500.

25. See "Procedures of the People's Bank of China for the Establishment of Representative Offices in China by Overseas and Foreign Financial Institutions" (1983), in CCH, para. 7–540(4).

26. See Financial Representative Office Regulations (1983), Article 8.

27. See "Procedures of the People's Bank of China for Controls Relating to Establishment of Representative Offices in China by Foreign Banking Institutions" (1991), in CCH, para. 7–542.

28. See "Regulations of the PRC on the Management of Foreign Funded Financial Institutions" (1994), in *China Economic News*, Apr. 18, 1994, p. 6.

29. See Henry R. Zheng, "The Special Economic Zones and Coastal Cities," in Streng & Wilcox, eds., *Doing Business in China*, Chapter 20.

30. See Constitution of the People's Republic of China (1982), Article 18.

31. By 1993, China had concluded BITs with over ten foreign countries. A Sino–U.S. BIT remained elusive, whereas a Sino–Canadian BIT was under negotiation.

32. By 1985 U.S.$3 billion had been pledged in foreign investment. See Pomfret, *Investing in China*, p. 54. The actual growth rate of pledged investment in EJVs soared to 463 percent in 1984. Pearson, *Joint Ventures*, p. 74.

33. See Erin McGuire Endean, "China's Foreign Commercial Relations", in Joint Economic Committee of U.S. Congress, ed., *China's Economic Dilemmas in the 1990s: The Problems of Reforms, Modernization, and Interdependence* (Washington, D.C.: U.S. Government Printing Office, 1991), p. 761.

34. Perhaps the most publicized case concerning the foreign exchange problems of an equity joint venture was the Beijing–Jeep project. See generally, Jim Mann, *Beijing Jeep: The Short, Unhappy Romance of American Business in China* (New York: Simon and Schuster, 1989).

35. See "State Council Measures For the Encouragement of Foreign Investment" (1986), in CCH, para. 13–509.

36. These included the following measures, all in *Zhongguo guli wai shang touze fagui xuanbian* (Compilation of laws and regulations of China on encouraging foreign investment) (Beijing: University of Politics and Law Press, 1987).
    1. Labor Ministry Regulations Concerning Autonomy in the Hiring of Personnel and in Salaries, Insurance and Expenses, Welfare Funds of Foreign Investment Enterprises (Nov. 26, 1986);
    2. PRC Customs Methods for Administration of Materials and Things Imported by Foreign Investment Enterprises as Needed to Fulfill Goods Export Contracts (Nov. 24, 1986);
    3. Bank of China Methods for Loans of Renminbi Secured by Foreign Exchange (Dec. 11, 1986);
    4. MOFERT Methods on the Purchase and Export of Domestic Produces by Foreign Investment Enterprises to Balance Income and Expenditures of Foreign Exchange (Jan. 20, 1987);
    5. MOFERT Implementing Procedures for Applications by Foreign Investment Enterprises for Import and Export Licenses (Jan. 24, 1987);
    6. MOFERT Implementing Rules for Examination and Confirmation of Export Enterprises and Technologically Advanced Enteprises with Foreign Investment (Jan. 27, 1987);
    7. Ministry of Finance Procedures for Implementation of Tax Preferences Contained in the State Council Provisions for the Encouragement of Foreign Investment (Jan. 30, 1987);
    8. Bank of China Methods for Loans to Foreign Investment Enterprises (Apr. 4, 1987);
    9. State Planning Commission Measures Relating to Import Substitution by Products Manufactured by Sino-Foreign Joint Ventures (Oct. 1987);
    10. State Economic Commission Measures Relating to Substitution of Mechanical and Electrical Products Manufactured by Sino-Foreign Joint Ventures (Oct. 1987).

37. A partial listing, including measures enacted in Fujian, Shandong, Liaoning, Guizhou, Jiangsu, Heilongjiang, Jilin, Yunnan, Guangxi, and Guangdong Provinces appears in pp. 159–95. Also see, for example, municipal regulations for Beijing (in *Beijing ribao*, Nov. 16, 1986, p. 2); Shanghai (in *Wenhui bao*, Oct. 25, 1986); Guangzhou (in *China Economic News*, July 6, 1987, p. 5, July 13, 1987, p. 7, and July 20, 1987, p. 9).

38. The 22 Articles specifically emphasized "technologically advanced" and "export-oriented" enterprises. Also see "Implementing Rules for Examination and Confirmation of Export Enterprises and Technologically Advanced Enterprises With Foreign Investment" (1987), in *China Economic News*, Nov. 7, 1987, p. 9, and Pitman B. Potter, "Seeking Special Status," in *China Business Review*, March-April, 1988, p. 36. These rules have recently been amended. See "Supplement to Implementary Rules of MOFERT for Examination and Confirmation of Export Enterprises and Technologically Advanced Enterprises with Foreign Investment" (1992), in *China Economic News*, No. 19, 1992, p. 7.

39. See "Company Law of the People's Republic of China" (hereafter "PRC Company Law"), in *China Economic News*, Supplement no. 2, March 7, 1994. A number of preliminary analyses have emerged addressing this legislation, including Preston

Torbert, "Broadening the Scope of Investment," in *The China Business Review*, May-June 1994, p. 48, and David Ho, "China's New Company Law: Something Concrete to Go By," in *East Asian Executive Reports*, Feb. 1994, p. 9.

40. See "Draft Corporate Law Submitted," *FBIS Daily Report—China*, Feb. 16, 1993, p. 29; and "Speech by Qiao Shi at Closing of NPC," *FBIS Daily Report—China*, Apr. 1, 1993, p. 22. Among the sources from which many of the Company Law's provisions were drawn are the Provisional Regulations of Shenzhen Municipality on Companies Limited by Shares (Mar. 17, 1992), reprinted in *China Law & Practice*, May 7, 1992, at p. 12 and the "Interim Provisions on the Management of the Issuing and Trading of Stocks," (in *China Economic News*, June 7, 1993, p. 7, June 14, 1993, p. 7, and June 21, 1993, p. 8).

41. Erin McGuire Endean, "China's Foreign Commercial Relations," in Joint Economic Committee of U.S. Congress, ed., *China's Economic Dilemmas in the 1990s: The Problems of Reforms, Modernization, and Interdependence* (Washington, D.C.: U.S. Government Printing Office, 1991), p. 761.

42. Ibid.

43. "China Data," *China Business Review*, May-June, 1992, p. 49.

44. "China Data," *China Business Review*, May-June, 1993, p. 57.

45. See "Statistical Communique of the State Statistical Bureau of the PRC on the 1993 National Economic and Social Development," in *China Economic News*, Supplement no. 3, Mar. 14, 1994, p. 5.

46. During 1992 the gap was $57.2 billion contracted/$10.1 billion used (see "Analysis of China's Use of Foreign Funds for 1992," *China Economic News*, May 24, 1993, p. 11), during 1993 the gap was $76.2 billion contracted/U.S.$36.77 billion used (see 1993 Statistical Communique, p. 5).

47. See, for example, "MOFTEC Spokesman's News Conference," in *FBIS Daily Report—China*, Jul. 27, 1993, p. 26.

48. See David Denny, "Provincial Economic Differences Diminished in the Decade of Reform," in Joint Economic Committee of U.S. Congress, ed., *China's Economic Dilemmas in the 1990s: The Problems of Reforms, Modernization, and Interdependence* (Washington, D.C.: U.S. Government Printing Office, 1991), pp. 186, 201.

49. See, for example, Graham E. Johnson, "Changing Horizons for Regional Development: Continuity and Transformation in Hong Kong and Its Hinterland: 1950s to 1990s" (unpublished paper presented to "Workshop on Hong Kong Guangdong Integration," University of British Columbia, 1992).

50. See, for example, R. Yin-Wang Kwok and Alvin So, "Hong Kong Guangdong Interaction: Joint Enterprise of Market Capitalism and State Socialism" (unpublished paper presented to "Workshop on Hong Kong Guangdong Integration," University of British Columbia, 1992).

51. See generally, Lee A. Brudvig, "The Fifth Dragon," in *China Business Review*, July-August, 1993, p. 14.

52. See generally, Pitman B. Potter, "The Role of Law in Inducing Foreign Investment into the PRC" (1990 Institute Issue Paper, 1992).

53. See "Zhu Rongji Addresses Finance, Tax Meetings" and "Comments on Financial Order," in *FBIS Daily Report—China*, Jul. 26, 1993, pp. 39 and 41.

54. See FECL, Article 6.

55. Compare 1983 Financial Representative Office Regulations, Article 8 with "Im-

plementing Regulations for the Joint Venture Law of the PRC" (1983, rev. 1986), in CCH, para. 6–550, Article 24. Virtually every bank representative office in China that I know of has had to pay foreign enterprise income taxes despite compliance with regulatory prohibitions against the pursuit of profit-making activities.

56. Compare 22 Articles, Article 15, with "Shanghai Municipality, Sino-Foreign Equity Joint Venture Labor Union Regulations" (1989), in *China Law and Practice*, Feb. 26, 1990, p. 52, Articles 6 and 8.

57. See, for example, "Zhuguan bumen neng shanzi huan heying qiye jingli ma?" (Can the department in charge exceed its authority and replace the manager of a joint venture enterprise?), in Zhang Huilong, *Shewai jingji fa anlijiexi* (Analysis of foreign economic law cases) (Beijing: Youth Publishing, 1990), p. 245.

58. See "Yi qi hezuo jingying qiye hetong jiufen an" (A case of a dispute over a cooperative joint venture contract), in Qi Tianchang, *Hetong anli pingxi* (Critical analysis of contract cases) (Beijing: University of Politics and Law Press, 1991), pp. 416–22.

59. See "The Council's Investment Initiative," *China Business Review*, Sept.-Oct., 1992, p. 6, where problems with "lack of uniformity and consistency in interpreting and implementing rules and regulation" were prominently cited.

60. See Patrick E. Tyler, "Chinese End Austerity Drive in Favor of Yet More Growth," in the *New York Times*, Nov. 23, 1993, Section A, pg. 1, col. 1.

61. See "Provisional Regulations of the PRC State Council Concerning Reduction and Elimination of Enterprise Tax and Industrial and Commercial Consolidated Tax in the Special Economic Zones and 14 Coastal Cities" (1984), in CCH, para. 70–845.

62. See, for example, "Wai shang touzezhe de fuyin—'er shi er tiao' you na xie guiding" ("Glad tidings for foreign business investors—the '22 Articles' have those provisions"), in Zhang Huilong, *Shewai jingji fa*, p. 256, wherein an effort to trumpet the benefits of the 22 Articles reveals instead the extent to which these provisions are replete with ambiguity and potential enforcement problems.

63. For example, the provisions in the 22 Articles permitting foreign investment enterprises to access the domestic market in order to balance foreign exchange permitted domestic sales to be approved on a case-by-case basis and only after the FIE was already in operation, thus preventing effective foreign exchange planning by the foreign investor. Although the impact of the import substitution provision has been significantly diminished by foreign exchange reform, and by general policies on market access, the example remains instructive to indicate perceived substantive defects in the 22 Articles.

64. Attitudes of foreign business in China are derived from numerous informal conversations conducted since 1985, and particularly during 1991–93. For additional discussion of business attitudes, see "The Council's Investment Initiative," *China Business Review*, Sept.-Oct., 1992, p. 6.

65. See generally, John L. Davie, "China's International Trade and Finance," in Joint Economic Committee of U.S. Congress, ed., *China's Economy Looks Toward the Year 2000* (Washington, D.C.: U.S. Gov't Printing Office, 1986), p. 311; Albert Keidel, "The Cyclical Pattern of China's Economic Reforms," in Joint Economic Committee of U.S. Congress, ed., *China's Economic Dilemmas in the 1990s: The Problems of Reforms, Modernization, and Interdependence* (Washington, D.C.: U.S. Gov't Printing Office, 1991), p. 119; and Samuel P. S. Ho and Ralph W.

Huenemann, *China's Open Door Policy: The Quest for Foreign Technology & Capital* (Vancouver: UBC Press, 1984).

66. See generally, Lee Zinzer, "The Performance of China's Economy," in Joint Economic Committee of U.S. Congress, ed., *China's Economic Dilemmas in the 1990s: The Problems of Reforms, Modernization, and Interdependence*, p. 102 at p. 109, et seq.

67. See WFOE Law, Article 5.

68. See generally, Timothy Steinhardt, "If the BIT Fits: The Proposed Bilateral Investment Treaty between the United States and the People's Republic of China," 2 *J. Chinese Law* 405 (1988).

69. See "State Council Investment in Retailing Provisions," in *China Law and Practice*, Mar. 25, 1993, p. 43.

70. The language used in the Joint Venture Law Article 1 ("the PRC permits foreign enterprises . . . to incorporate themselves, within the territory of the PRC, into joint ventures with Chinese companies . . . subject to authorization by the Chinese government . . . ") and Article 2 ("[a]ll activities of a joint venture shall be governed by the laws . . . of the PRC . . . ") underscored the government's concern with control and limitation of the activities of Joint Venture Laws (JVs). Also see Peng Zhen, "Explanation of the Seven Draft Laws" (1979), in which Peng discusses the government's purposes in permitting joint ventures as tied to the import of technology and capital.

71. See Joint Venture Law Implementing Regulations, Article 3, in which language concerning the imperative to promote the development of the Chinese economy reveals the instrumentalism at work in the government's conception of the purpose of joint ventures. The separate standards imposed on joint ventures as opposed to domestic enterprises is underscored by the provisions of Article 4 concerning the importance of achieving economic results, thus the limited willingness to "permit" joint ventures (Joint Venture Law, Article 1) is conditioned on economic performance.

Chapter 4

1. For a more thorough discussion on this point, see Stanley B. Lubman, "Technology Transfer to China: Policies, Law and Practice," in Michael J. Moser (ed.), *Foreign Trade, Investment and the Law in the People's Republic of China* (Hong Kong, Oxford, New York: Oxford University Press), 1984.

2. See generally, U.S. Congress Office of Technology Assessment, "Technology Transfer to China" (Washington, D.C.: U.S. Government Printing Office, 1987), pp. 21–35.

3. See generally, Office of Technology Assessment, "Technology Transfer to China," pp. 36–68.

4. See "Regulations on the Administration of Technology Import Contracts of the People's Republic of China" (Technology Import Regulations) (1985), in CCH, para. 5–570. Although the State Council's 1985 regulations on technology transfer contracts were often cited by regulatory officials, these measures were intended mainly to establish the basic rights and duties that derive from technology transfers between Chinese enterprises. See "Provisional Regulations on Technology Transfer" (1985), in CCH, para. 19–536. These provisions do not make reference to foreign parties, but do make particular reference in Article 3 to the Economic Contract Law,

which specifically excludes foreign parties for its scope. These measures were largely (albeit not formally) displaced by the Law of the PRC on Technology Contracts (in CCH, Para 5–577), which in Article 2 specifically excluded foreign parties from its scope.

5. See Technology Import Regulations, Article 2. This requirement is somewhat contradictory, in the sense that "advanced" is generally interpreted to mean state of the art, while "appropriate" means the highest level usable under local conditions. In China, it is often the case that "advanced" technology may not be appropriate for use under local conditions.

6. See "Detailed Rules for the Implementation of the Administrative Regulations of the People's Republic of China on Technology Import Contracts" (hereafter, "Technology Import Implementing Rules") (1988), in CCH, para. 5–573.

7. See Technology Import Regulations, Article 9, and Technology Import Implementing Rules, Articles 14 and 15.

8. See Technology Import Regulations, Article 6, and Technology Import Implementing Rules, Articles 9 and 11.

9. The appropriate reviewing authority is determined by the location and capital value of the project. See Stanley B. Lubman, "Technology Transfer to China: Policies, Law and Practice," in Michael J. Moser (ed.), *Foreign Trade, Investment and the Law in the People's Republic of China* (Hong Kong, Oxford, New York: Oxford University Press, 1984), at section 304[4].

10. Technology Import Implementing Rules, Article 6.

11. Technology Import Implementing Rules, Article 18.

12. See Joint Venture Law, Article 5.

13. See Joint Venture Law Implementing Regulations, Article 44.

14. See Joint Venture Law Implementing Regulations, Article 28.

15. See Cooperative Enterprise Law (1988), WFOE Law (1986).

16. See State Council Measures For the Encouragement of Foreign Investment.

17. See State Council Implementing Rules for the Confirmation and Examination of Export-Oriented and Technologically Advanced Enterprises with Foreign Investment, Article 4. Also see Pitman B. Potter, "Seeking Special Status," *China Business Review*, March-April, 1988, p. 36.

18. Ibid.

19. See "Trademark Law of the PRC," in CCH, para. 11–500. For a Chinese-language text of the 1963 regulations, see "Shangbiao guanli tiaoli" (Administrative regulations for trademarks), in Trademark Office of the State Administration for Industry and Commerce, *Shangbiao fagui ziliao xuanbian* (Selected laws and regulations and materials on trademark) (Beijing: Law Publishers, 1985), p. 52.

20. See Jesse T. Chang and Charles Conroy, "Trademark in the People's Republic of China," in Michael J. Moser, *Foreign Trade, Investment and the Law in the People's Republic of China* (Hong Kong, Oxford, New York: Oxford University Press, 1984), p. 269.

21. See "Detailed Rules for the Implementation of the Trademark Law of the People's Republic of China" (1983, rev. 1988), in CCH, para. 11–510.

22. See Trademark Law Implementing Regulations (as amended), Article 9.

23. See Trademark Law, Article 8. The prohibited marks follow broadly those listed in the Paris Convention for the Protection of Industrial Property, however note sub-

paragraphs (g) and (h) disallowing marks having "exaggeration and deceit in advertising," or that are "detrimental to socialist morals or customs, or having another unhealthy influence."

24. See "Administrative Litigation Law of the PRC" (1989), in CCH, para. 19–558.

25. See Trademark Law, Articles 6 and 31.

26. See Trademark Law, Article 38.

27. Paris Convention for the Protection of Industrial Property, in *International Legal Materials*, vol. 6, p. 981 (1968).

28. See "Patent Law of the PRC" (1985, rev. 1993), in CCH, para. 11–600; and "Implementation Regulations of the Patent Law of the PRC" (hereafter, "Patent Implementation Regulations"), in CCH, para. 11–603. The Patent Law was promulgated on March 12, 1984, but it did not become effective until April 1, 1985, when the implementing regulations as well went into effect.

29. See Patent Law, Articles 2 and 22.

30. See Zheng Chengsi (with Michael Pendleton), *Chinese Intellectual Property and Technology Transfer Law* (London: Sweet & Maxwell, 1987), pp. 65–66.

31. See Patent Law, Article 24.

32. See Patent Law, Article 44. However, judicial review is available in connection with decisions by the patent administration authorities concerning disputes between private parties over inter alia the right to apply for a patent. See "Patent Administrative Authority Adjudicating Patent Disputes Procedures," in *China Law and Practice*, May 7, 1990, p. 40.

33. See Patent Law, Articles 51–52.

34. See Patent Law, Article 62.

35. See "Beijing Municipality Patent Dispute Mediation Procedures" (1988), in *China Law and Practice*, Aug. 21, 1989, p. 54; "Shanghai Patent Dispute Mediation Tentative Procedures" (1988), in *China Law and Practice*, Aug. 21, 1989, p. 59. These were followed by national regulations. See "Patent Administrative Authority Adjudicating Patent Disputes Procedures" (1989).

36. See Agreement on Trade Relations Between the U.S.A. and P.R.C. (1979), in TIAS 9630, 31 U.S.T. 4651, Article VI.

37. Under the 1988 Omnibus Trade and Competitiveness Act, 19 U.S.C. 2411–2416 (1982 & Supp. IV 1986), the USTR is required, pursuant to Section 301, to designate countries violating international intellectual property standards as priority countries for the implementation of trade sanctions.

38. See Pitman B. Potter, "Bettering Protection for Intellectual Property," *The China Business Review*, July-August, 1989, p. 27.

39. See "Copyright Law of the PRC" (1990), in CCH, para. 11–700; "Detailed Rules for the Implementation of the Copyright Law of the PRC" (1991), in CCH, para. 11–702.

40. See Copyright Law, Article 22.

41. Copyright Implementing Rules, Article 25.

42. See Memorandum of Understanding between the Government of the People's Republic of China and the Government of the United States of America on the Protection of Intellectual Property (1992), Article 3. Author's copy.

43. See Berne Convention on the Protection of Literary and Artistic Works, Article 18(1), WIPO Doc. 287(E).

44. See Copyright Law, Article 53.
45. See "Computer Software Protection Regulations," in *China Law and Practice*, Aug. 19, 1991, p. 55.
46. See Patent Law of the PRC (as amended, 1993), Article 45.
47. See Administrative Protection of Pharmaceutical Regulations (1993), in *China Law and Practice*, Mar. 25, 1993, p. 37.
48. See "Trademark Law of the PRC" (as amended, 1993), in CCH, para. 11–500.
49. See Denis Fred Simon, "China's Acquisition and Assimilation of Foreign Technology: Beijing's Search for Excellence," in Joint Economic Committee of U.S. Congress, ed., *China's Economic Dilemmas in the 1990s: The Problems of Reforms, Modernization, and Interdependence* (Washington, D.C.: U.S. Gov't. Printing Office, 1991), p. 575.
50. See Pitman B. Potter, "Technology Transfers to China," in Zhang Lixing, Dorinda Dallmeyer, Robert K. Patterson, and Thomas J. Shoenbaum, eds., *Chinese Economic Law and Selected Comparisons from the Pacific Rim* (Athens, GA: University of Georgia, 1988).
51. See Office of the United States Trade Representative, *China IPR Fact Sheet* (1992).
52. See, for example, the 22 Articles, which provide special incentives for "advanced technology enterprises."
53. Compare "Supplement to MOFERT Implementing Rules for Examination and Confirmation of Export Enterprises and Export-Oriented Enterprises," Article 5, in *China Economic News*, no. 19, 1992, p. 7 with "MOFERT Implementing Rules for Examination and Confirmation of Export Enterprises and Export-Oriented Enterprises," Article 4, in *China Economic News*, no. 7, 1987, p. 9.
54. See U.S. China Business Council, "Recommendations on Amendment of the China Patent Law" (1988), author's copy; Pitman B. Potter, "Bettering Protection for Intellectual Property."
55. See Technology Import Regulations, Technology Import Implementing Rules. For discussion of these provisions, see Pitman B. Potter, "Technology Transfers to China."
56. Numerous personal communications in Beijing, Shanghai, and Hong Kong during 1987–89 and 1991–93. See Appendix C for a partial list of sources interviewed on a confidential basis during 1991–93. Also see "The Council's Investment Initiative," in *The China Business Review*, Sept.-Oct. 1992, p. 6; Sheila Tefft, "U.S. Message to China: Punish Potent Pirates," in *Christian Science Monitor*, Oct. 28, 1994.
57. For examples of IPR infringements, see Chen Chia-yao, "Supergroup Produces Pirated Laser Discs," in *Yi Chou Kan* (HK), Feb. 25, 1994, p. 38, reprinted in *FBIS Daily Report-China*, Mar. 2, 1994, p. 3.
58. See, for example, Regulations of Beijing and Shanghai municipalities on resolving patent disputes, which make extensive use of administrative measures.
59. See Patent Law of the PRC, Article 60; Trademark Law of the PRC, Article 39; and Copyright Law of the PRC, Article 46.
60. For example, the imperial examination system was based on rote memorization of Confucian classics. See Ho Ping-ti, *The Ladder of Success in Imperial China* (New York: 1962). The training of artists and calligraphers on the other hand involved the ritual copying of old masters. See Mai-mai Sze, Tr., ed., *The Mustard Seed Garden of Painting* (Princeton: Princeton University Press, 1963); Shen Y. C. Fu with Jan

Stuart, *Challenging the Past: The Paintings of Chang Dai-Chien* (Washington, D.C.: Smithsonian Institution, 1991).

61. See generally, Jerome A. Cohen, "China's Changing Constitution," in *The China Quarterly*, vol. 76 (1978).
62. See Constitution of the PRC, 1982, Article 13.
63. For Example, the Joint Venture Law (1990) makes specific reference to promoting international economic cooperation and technological exchange. Also see generally, Guo Shoukang, "Technology Transfer," in Rui Mu, ed., *Chinese Foreign Economic Law*.
64. See Patent Law 9 (as amended), Chapter VI.
65. See "Memorandum of Understanding between the Government of the People's Republic of China and the Government of the United States of America on the Protection of Intellectual Property" (1992), Article 1 (I) (d).
66. See "White Paper in Intellectual Property Rights Published," in *FBIS Daily Report—China*, June 16, 1994, p. 32. Also see "China Defends Copyright System Ahead of U.S. Sanction Threat," Agence France Presse English Wire, June 16, 1994, in *China News Digest* (electronic media), June 16, 1994.

Chapter 5

1. See "Provisional Regulations of the People's Republic of China Governing Foreign Exchange Control" (hereafter "Foreign Exchange Regs"), in CCH, para. 8–550. The SAEC is an administrative organ under the supervision of the People's Bank of China (PBOC), and is responsible for controlling foreign exchange. See Carsten Holz, *The Role of Central Banking in China's Economic Reforms* (Ithaca: Cornell University Press, 1992), pp. 68 et seq. The Bank of China is a specialized bank, supervised and monitored by the PBOC and the State Council, responsible for the management of foreign exchange and the provision of loans and export credits to foreign enterprises and joint ventures. See generally, Che-ning Liu, "From Cashiers to Banks: Banking Reform in the People's Republic of China and the Emergence of Banks as Financial Intermediaries," in 6 *China L. Rep.* 103 (1990).
2. See Joint Venture Law, Articles 8 and 9.
3. See "Rules for the Implementation of Foreign Exchange Controls Relating to Enterprises with Overseas Chinese Capital, Enterprises with Foreign Capital, and Chinese-Foreign Equity Joint Ventures" (hereafter "Foreign Exchange Control Implementing Rules"), in CCH, para. 8–670.
4. See Joint Venture Law Implementing Rules, Article 64.
5. See Joint Venture Law Implementing Rules, Article 75.
6. See Margaret Pearson, *Joint Ventures in the People's Republic of China* (Princeton: Princeton University Press, 1991), pp. 135–38.
7. See "Regulations Concerning the Issue of Balancing Foreign Exchange Receipts and Disbursements by Joint Ventures Using Chinese and Foreign Investment" (hereafter "Forex Balancing Regulations"), in *Collection of Laws and Regulations of the People's Republic of China Concerning Foreign Economic Affairs*, vol. 5, p. 106.
8. See State Council Provisions on Encouraging Foreign Investment. Also see Virginia Davis and Carlos Yi, "Balancing Foreign Exchange," in *China Business Review*, March-April 1992, p. 14.

9. See "MOFERT Measures for Foreign Investment Enterprises Purchasing Domestic Products for Export to Achieve a Balance of Foreign Exchange Income and Expenditure" (1987), in CCH, para. 13–526.

10. See "Administrative Provisions on the Calculation and Settling of Prices in Foreign Currency within China by Enterprises with Foreign Investment" (hereafter "1989 Forex Pricing Regulations"), in CCH, para. 8–730.

11. Compare 1989 Forex Pricing Regulations with "Measures Relating to the Import Substitution by Products Manufactured by Chinese Foreign Equity Joint Ventures and Chinese Foreign Cooperative Joint Ventures"(1987), in *China Economic News*, Nov. 8, 1987, p. 7.

12. In fact both the import substitution regulations and the 1989 Forex Pricing Regulations tended to evolve into barriers to domestic market access, as they were increasingly interpreted not as a potential avenue for foreign exchange balancing but rather as rigid prerequisites to market access. Under the U.S.–China Market Access Agreement of 1992 China agreed to abolish its import substitution regulations.

13. Article 15 of the 22 Articles authorized foreign investment enterprises to engage in the mutual adjustment of their foreign exchange surpluses and deficits.

14. See Virginia Davis and Carlos Yi, "Balancing Foreign Exchange," *China Business Review*, March-April 1992, p. 14.

15. See "Announcement of the People's Bank of China on Further Reforming the Foreign Exchange Management System" (Dec. 28, 1993), in *China Economic News*, Jan. 10, 1994, p. 9.

16. "Provisional Regulations on the Management of Settlement, Sales and Payment of Foreign Exchange," in *China Economic News*, Apr. 25, 1994, p. 6 and May 2, 1994, p. 7.

17. See generally, "China's First Batch of Bank Laws Soon Come Out," in *China Economic News*, Jan. 3, 1994, p. 2, which discusses the pending enactment of a Banking Law and a Central Bank Law that will in effect separate the functions of commercial banking and central banking for China's state banks.

18. See generally, Timothy A. Gelatt and Richard D. Pomp, "Tax Aspects of Doing Business with the People's Republic of China," in 22 *Columbia J. of Transnational L.* 421 (1984).

19. See "Income Tax Law of the PRC for Joint Ventures With Chinese and Foreign Investment," in *China's Foreign Economic Legislation Vol. I* (Beijing: Foreign Languages Press, 1982), pp. 36–44; "Detailed Rules for the Implementation of the Income Tax Law of the PRC for Joint Ventures With Chinese and Foreign Investment," in *China's Foreign Economic Legislation Vol. I* (Beijing: Foreign Languages Press, 1982), pp. 45–55.

20. See Foreign Enterprise Income Tax Law of the PRC (1981), in *China's Foreign Economic Legislation Vol. I* (Beijing: Foreign Languages Press, 1982), pp. 55–63; Detailed Rules for the Implementation of the Foreign Enterprise Income Tax Law of the PRC (1982), in *China's Foreign Economic Legislation Vol. II* (Beijing: Foreign Languages Press, 1982), pp. 64–74.

21. The tax surcharge equal to 10 percent of the taxable income, not the assessed tax due as provided for under the JV Tax Law. Compare Foreign Enterprise Income Tax Law, Article 4 with JV Tax Law, Article 3.

22. One requirement for obtaining a tax reduction is that the enterprise be engaged in

small-scale production or operations and have a low profit rate. See Foreign Enterprise Tax Law, Article 7.

23. See "Interim Provisions on the Reduction and Exemption of Enterprise Income Tax and Consolidated Industrial and Commercial Tax in Special Economic Zones and 14 Coastal Cities" (1984) (1984 SEZ/ETDZ Tax Reduction Regulations), in CCH, para. 70–845.

24. See, for example, Henry R. Zheng, "The Special Economic Zones and Coastal Cities," in William P. Streng and Allen C. Wilcox, eds., *Doing Business in China* (Irvington-on-Hudson, NY: Transnational Juris, looseleaf), Chapter 20.

25. See "Income Tax Law of the People's Republic of China for Enterprises with Foreign Investment and Foreign Enterprises" (1991), CCH, para. 32–505.

26. Compare UFETL, with 1984 SEZ/ETDZ Tax Reduction Regulations.

27. See UFETL Implementing Rules, Article 67.

28. See UFETL Implementing Rules, Article 68.

29. See UFETL, Article 13.

30. See UFETL, Articles 22 through 27.

31. For a text of the 1980 law and regulations, see "Individual Income Tax Law of the People's Republic of China" and "Rules for the Implementation of the Individual Income Tax Law of the People's Republic of China," both in *China's Foreign Economic Legislation* (Beijing: Foreign Languages Press, 1982), pp. 75 and 85, respectively. The revised texts appear in "Individual Income Tax Law of the People's Republic of China" (1980, 1993), in CCH, para. 30–500; "Implementing Regulations for the Individual Income Tax Law of the People's Republic of China" (1994), in CCH, para. 30–305. For a general discussion of these measures, see Pitman B. Potter, "Taxation of Foreign Individuals," in William P. Streng and Allen Wilcox, eds., *Doing Business in China* (Irvington-on-Hudson, NY: Transnational Juris Publishers, looseleaf).

32. For a useful review of the amendments to the Individual Income Tax Law, see Timothy Gelatt, "China's New Individual Income Tax Law: Implications for Foreign Business," in *East Asian Executive Reports*, November 1993, p. 1.

33. Article 2 of the IITL provides that individual income tax shall be levied on income derived from wages and salaries, royalties, and compensation for personal services (for example, accounting, consulting, medical and legal services rendered, etc.); interest, dividends, and bonuses, rental income; and other income specified by the Ministry of Finance. The definitions of these kinds of income are set forth in the IITL Implementing Regulations.

34. See Regulations on Industrial and Commercial Consolidated Tax (1958) (Zhonghua renmin gongheguo gong shang tong yi shui tiaoli), in State Taxation Bureau, *Zhongguo she wai shuishou fagui ji* (Volume of PRC laws and regulations on foreign taxation) (Beijing: Finance and Tax Publishers, 1989), p. 217; Detailed Rules for the Implementation of the Regulations on Industrial and Commercial Consolidated Tax (1958) (Zhonghua renmin gongheguo gong shang tong yi shui tiaoli shixing xize), in State Taxation Bureau, *Zhongguo she wai shuishou fagui ji* (Volume of PRC laws and regulations on foreign taxation) (Beijing: Finance and Tax Publishers, 1989), p. 228. Also see Alex Easson and Li Jinyan, "The Evolution of the Tax System in the People's Republic of China," in 23 *Stanford J. Int'l L.* 399 (1987).

35. See "Draft Regulations of the PRC on Value Added Tax" (Zhonghua renmin gon-

gheguo zengzhishui tiaoli) (1984), in Beijing Taxation Society and Beijing Economics Institute eds., *Na shui zixun shouce* (Handbook of consultation on payment of tax) (Beijing: Beijing Publishers, 1986), p. 561.

36. See "Guanyu dui wai heze jingying qiye, hezuo shengchan hezuo jingying qiye he ge shang duli jingying qiye zhengshou gongshang tongyi shui wenti de tongzhi" (Notice concerning questions of the imposition of ICCT to joint ventures, cooperative production and cooperative managed enterprises, and independent enterprises), in State Taxation Bureau, *Shui fa da chuan* (Encyclopedia of tax law) (Beijing: Finance and Economy Publishers, 1989), p. 524.

37. "Zhonghua renmin honghe guo caizhengbu dui waiguo qiye changzhu daibiao jigou zheng shou gongshang tongyi shui, qiye suode shui de zanxing guiding" (Provisional regulations of the Ministry of Finance on the imposition of ICCT and foreign enterprise tax on foreign representative offices) (1985), in Li Bichang, ed., *Zhongguo dui wai shui shou falu zhidu* (China's legal system for taxation of foreigners) (Beijing: Law Publishers, 1988), p. 279.

38. See "Provisional Regulations of the PRC State Council Concerning Reduction and Elimination of Enterprise Tax and Industrial and Commercial Consolidated Tax in the Special Economic Zones and 14 Coastal Cities" (1984), in CCH, para. 70–845.

39. See "Decision on the Use of Interim Regulations Concerning Value-Added Taxes, Consumption Taxes, and Business Taxes on FFEs and Foreign Enterprises" (1993), in *China Economic News*, Jan. 31, 1994, p. 7.

40. See "Provisional Regulations of the PRC on Value-Added Tax," in *China Economic News*, Jan. 3, 1994, p. 9. Also see VAT Implementing Rules in "Special Supplement on Taxation," in *China Economic News*, Supplement no. 1, Jan. 31, 1994, p. 2. The 1993 VAT replaced the 1984 version. See 1993 VAT Regulations, Article 29.

41. See "Provisional Regulations of the PRC on Consumption Taxes," in *China Economic News*, Jan. 17, 1994, p. 7. Also see Consumption Tax Implementing Regulations in "Special Supplement on Taxation," in *China Economic News*, Supplement no. 1, Jan. 31, 1994, p. 6.

42. See "Provisional Regulations of the PRC on Business Taxes," in *China Economic News*, Jan. 17, 1994, p. 10. Also see Business Tax Implementing Regulations in "Special Supplement on Taxation," in *China Economic News*, Supplement no. 1, Jan. 31, 1994, p. 9.

43. See "Provisional Regulations of the PRC on Land Value-Added Taxes," in *China Economic News*, Jan. 17, 1994, p. 7.

44. Although they are subject to some debate, the new taxes will undoubtedly affect foreign business, if only because they reflect more clearly the realities of business transactions in contemporary China than did the ICCT, which was a hallmark of China's 1950s planned economy. See generally, "Beijing to Give Tax Rebates to Foreign Companies Hurt by Tax Reform," *Associated Press*, Jan. 12, 1994 reprinted in *China New Digest* (electronic medium), Jan. 13, 1994; and "Government's New Tax Rules Will Hit Foreign Investors," *South China Morning Post*, Jan. 12, 1994, reprinted in *China New Digest* (electronic medium), Jan. 13, 1994.

45. See "Law of the PRC to Administer the Levying and Collection of Taxes" (1992) (hereafter "Tax Administration Law"), in CCH, para. 30–545; "Detailed Rules for the Implementation of the Law of the People's Republic of China to Administer the

Levying and Collection of Taxes" (1993) (hereafter "Tax Administration Implementing Regulations"), in CCH, para. 30–355.

46. See "Provisional Regulations of the PRC Concerning the Administration of Tax Revenues and Tax Enforcement" (State Council Econ. Laws and Regs. Res. Center and Secretariat of the Soc'y for Res. in Chinese Econ. Law), *Zuixin jingji fagui* (Latest economic legislation) (Machinery Industry Publishers, 1987), pp. 116–24. A translation of these regulations appears in *The China Investment Guide*, 19.01 N.3, at 553–58.

47. See Tax Administration Law, Articles 32, et seq.; Tax Administration Implementing Rules, Chapter VI.

48. See Tax Administration Law, Chapter V; Tax Administration Implementing Rules, Chapter VII.

49. See Tax Administration Law, Article 56.

50. Ibid.

51. Ibid.

52. Ibid.

53. Ibid.

54. See "Xingzheng fuyi tiaoli," in *Fazhi ribao* (Legal system daily), Dec. 28, 1990, p. 2. See also Pitman B. Potter, "The Administrative Litigation Law of the PRC," in *Chinese Law and Government*, Fall 1991.

55. See "Regulations on Administrative Reconsideration in Taxation Matters" (1991). Also see Tax Administration Law, Article 60.

56. See generally, William P. Streng, "China's Income Tax Agreements," in William P. Streng and Allen D. Wilcox, eds., *Doing Business in China* (Irvington-on-Hudson, NY: Transnational Juris, looseleaf).

57. Agreement between the United States of America and People's Republic of China for the Avoidance of Double Taxation and Prevention of Tax Evasion with Respect to Income Taxes became effective on Jan. 1, 1987 (hereafter "U.S.- PRC Tax Treaty"). CCH Tax Treaties #1421. Also see generally, William P. Streng, "China's Income Tax Agreements," in Streng & Wilcox, *Doing Business in China*, Chapter 18.

58. See generally, Paul D. McKenzie, "Foreign Exchange and Joint Ventures with China: Short-term Strategies and Long-Term Prospects," 17 *Can. Bus. L. J.* 114 (1990).

59. See Robert Kleinberg, *China's "Opening" to the Outside World*, pp. 210, et seq. Also see ongoing comparison of official and swap center rates in *Canada China Business Forum* (Canada China Business Council).

60. See "Rules for the Implementation of Exchange Control Regulations Relating to Enterprises with Overseas Chinese Capital, Enterprises With Foreign Capital, and Sino–Foreign Joint Equity Ventures."

61. See 22 Articles, Article 14.

62. See, for example, Ministry of Finance: Tax Bureau and Treaty and Law Division, *Shewai shui fa zhishi* (Knowledge on foreign taxation law) (Beijing: 1987), p. 4.

63. Ibid. Also see Don R. Castleman, "Taxation in the People's Republic of China: The System and Its Function," 46 *Alb. L. Rev.* 776 (1982), pp. 787–88; also Alex Easson and Li Jinyan, "The Evolution of the Tax System of the PRC."

64. See Joint Venture Income Tax Law, Articles 5–6.

65. See SEZ/ETDZ Tax Reduction Regulations.

66. See, for example, "Shenzhen Special Economic Zone Supplemental Regulations on Reduction of Taxation on Enterprises" (1986), in CCH, para. 73–527.

67. See "Notice of the Beijing Tax Bureau on Reduction of Individual Income Tax" (1987), author's copy.

68. See 22 Articles, Articles 7–9.

69. See UFETL. Also see Wang Bingqian, "Explanation of the PRC Income Tax Law (Draft) for Foreign Enterprises and Enterprises with Foreign Investment," Apr. 2, 1991, in *FBIS Daily Report-China*, June 14, 1991, p. 113.

70. See generally, Li Bichang, ed., *Zhongguo dui wai shui shou falu zhidu* (China's legal system for taxation of foreigners) (Beijing: Law Publishers, 1988), at pp. 8–11. Also see Robert Kleinberg, *China's "Opening" to the Outside World*, pp. 112–16.

71. In his speech presenting the IITL to the PRC National People's Congress, Gu Ming explained that a major purpose of the IITL is as a tax on the incomes of foreigners in China: "In our country, because of carrying out the system of low wages the people's income is not high, and formerly we did not impose an individual income tax. However, following the development of the economy, the people who receive high incomes will steadily increase, and they should make as much of a contribution to the state as they can. Particularly as a result of the development in economic interchanges with foreign countries, persons of foreign nationality who are obtaining income in our country are increasing day by day. Overseas Chinese in our country are paying income taxes in accordance with the laws and regulations of their local countries. At the same time the number of people who are engaged in economic activity or other work abroad also is steadily increasing, and they all must pay income taxes according to the regulations of the country where they are located. In order to protect the economic interests of our country, on the basis of the principles of equality and mutual benefit, and according to the circumstances both domestically and internationally, and giving due attention to the customs and practices abroad, the draft IITL was drafted." See State Tax Bureau, ed., *Zhongguo shewai shui shou fa gui ji* (Compilation of Chinese Laws and Regulations on the Taxation of Income Relating to Foreign Matter) (Beijing: China Finance and Economy Printers, 1989), pp. 627–28. Also see Pitman B. Potter, "Taxation of Foreign Individuals," in William P. Streng and Allen D. Wilcox, *Doing Business in China* (Irvington-on-Hudson, NY: Transnational Juris Publishers, 1993).

72. See 22 Articles.

73. See 22 Articles, Articles 7–9.

74. See discussion of technology transfer in Chapter 4.

75. See, for example, "Move Against Local Tax Breaks," in *FBIS Daily Report-China*, July 26, 1993, p. 42; "Foreign-Related Tax System to Be Improved," in *FBIS Daily Report-China*, July 27, 1993, p. 27.

76. See Law of the PRC on Administration of Taxation, Article 1.

77. The Value-Added Tax enacted in 1993 in fact replaced the ICCT. However, an earlier value-added tax enacted in 1984 was often cited as the reason for exorbitant cost transfers by Chinese enterprises to foreign investment enterprises. See notes 35 and 40, and accompanying text.

78. See "Agreement between the Government of the United States of America and the

Government of the People's Republic of China for the Avoidance of Double Taxation and the Prevention of Tax Evasion with Respect To Taxes on Income."

79. See PRC, Administration of the Finances of Foreign Investment Enterprises Provisions (1992). Also see Law of the PRC on Administration of Taxation.

80. See "Move Against Local Tax Breaks," in which Finance Minister Liu Zhongli is quoted as saying that foreign-funded enterprises have been major tax evaders.

Chapter 6

1. See Foreign Economic Contract Law, Article 37.

2. In some circumstances, the laws of a third country may be applied. A full discussion of the choice of law rules that would affect decisions on selection of governing law is beyond the scope of this volume. For preliminary discussion, see generally, Christian Salbaing, "Dispute Settlement in China," in Streng and Wilcox, eds., *Doing Business in China* (Irvington-on-Hudson, NY: Transnational Juris Publishers, 1983), pp. 21–88 at pp. 21–41.

3. FECL, Article 5. Although many Chinese parties are reluctant to agree to foreign law to govern their transactions, this is gradually changing—even in smaller transactions.

4. Arbitration for domestic economic contracts is controlled by the "Regulations on Arbitration for Economic Contracts of the People's Republic of China," in CCH, para. 10–620.

5. Arbitration for maritime issues is controlled by the "Arbitration Rules of the China Maritime Arbitration Commission issued by the China Council for the Promotion of International Trade" (1988), in CCH, para. 10–545.

6. The procedures for resolving disputes were embodied in the "Provisional Rules of Procedure of the Foreign Trade Arbitration Commission" (hereafter "1956 FETAC Rules"), in Owen Nee, ed., *Commercial Business and Trade Laws, People's Republic of China*, Booklet no. 15, Nov. 1983, p. L.3.

7. This approach for resolving disputes is reflected in the "Agreement on Trade Relations between the U.S.A. and P.R.C." (1979), in 31 U.S.T. 4651.

8. See "Law (for Trial Implementation) of the PRC on Civil Procedure," (hereafter "Draft Civil Procedure Law"), Article 192, in *Selections From World Broadcasts*, Mar. 17, 1982, p. C/1.

9. See "Arbitration Provisions of the China International Economic and Trade Arbitration Commission" (1989) (1989 CIETAC Rules), in CCH, para. 10–505.

10. See 1989 CIETAC Rules, Article 1. FETAC was compelled to hear any case brought before it so long as the parties had entered into an arbitration agreement.

11. FETAC's jurisdiction was limited to disputes between Chinese and foreign parties. See 1956 FETAC Rules, Article 2.

12. See 1989 CIETAC Rules, Article 2.

13. See 1989 CIETAC Rules, Articles 18–20.

14. See Zhang Yuling, "Towards the UNCITRAL Model Law: A Chinese Perspective," in 11 *J. of Int'l Arb.* 87 at pp. 114 et seq. (1994).

15. See 1989 CIETAC Rules, Article 36. In a departure from the FETAC Rules, interim awards may be made by a majority of the arbitration tribunal under the 1989 CIETAC Rules, Article 95.

16. See Convention on the Recognition and Enforcement of Foreign Arbitral Awards, in

TIAS 6997, 330 UNTS 3; Notice Concerning the Enforcement of United Nations Convention on the Recognition and Enforcement of Foreign Arbitral Awards Acceded to by Our Country, PRC Supreme People's Court, Circular No. 5, April 10, 1987 (author's copy).

17. See Chen Dejun, "Report on the Amendment Draft of the Arbitration Rules of China International Economic and Trade Arbitration Commission" (unpublished), cited in Zhang Yulin, "Towards The UNCITRAL Model Law: A Chinese Perspective," in *Journal of International Arbitration*, vol. 11, no. 1, Mar. 1994, p. 87. Also see Stanley B. Lubman and Gregory C. Wajnowski, "International Commercial Dispute Resolution in China: A Practical Assessment," in *The American Review of International Arbitration*, vol. 4, no. 2, 1993, p. 107.

18. The organization of the People's Courts is set forth in the "Organic Law of the People's Courts of the People's Republic of China," in Yu Manking, ed., *A Full Translation of the Criminal Law Code and 3 Other Codes of the PRC* (Hong Kong: Great Earth Book Co., 1980), p. 111.

19. See "Civil Procedure Law of the People's Republic of China" (1991), in CCH, para. 19–200.

20. See CPL, Article 6. The 1982 Constitution of the People's Republic of China has a similar provision under Article 126.

21. These provisions are contained in Part 4 of the CPL and establish basic principles of reciprocity and supremacy of international agreements over domestic law concerning matters of arbitration, service of process, and judicial assistance.

22. CPL, Article 261.

23. For a more detailed discussion on the enforcement of foreign arbitral awards prior to China's accession to the New York Convention see Cheung, Andrew Kui-nung, "Enforcement of Foreign Arbitral Awards in the People's Republic of China," 34 *Am. J. Comp. Law* 295 (1986).

24. See, for example, 1979 U.S.–P.R.C. Trade Agreement, Article VIII, Section 3, which provides that the signatory parties are each obligated to ensure that arbitration awards be "recognized and enforced by their competent authorities where enforcement is sought, in accordance with applicable laws and regulations."

25. On December 2, 1986, the National People's Congress ratified the New York Convention and announced April 22, 1987, as the effective date.

26. See "Notice Concerning the Enforcement of United Nations Convention on the Recognition and Enforcement of Foreign Arbitral Awards Acceded to by Our Country," Supreme People's Court, Circular No. 5, April 10, 1987 (author's copy).

27. See Christian Salbaing, "Dispute Settlement in China," in Streng and Wilcox, *Doing Business in China*, Chapter 21 at para 21.05[5].

28. See generally, Zhang Yulin, "Towards The UNCITRAL Model Law: A Chinese Perspective," in *Journal of International Arbitration*, vol. 11, no. 1, Mar. 1994, p. 87. This has paralleled the increase in commercial disputes domestically in China. During the five years prior to 1993, the Chinese People's Courts handled some 8.9 million civil cases of first instance, which accounted for more than 60 percent of the total number of lawsuits brought and which saw an increase in the number of cases filed of nearly 10 percent per year. See "Court President Ren Jianxin Reports to [NPC] Session," *Xinhua* English service Mar. 22, 1993, in *FBIS Daily Report—China*, Mar. 23, 1993, p. 41.

29. See Christian Salbaing, "Dispute Settlement in China," pp. 21–55.
30. See Stanley B. Lubman, "Introduction," in Pitman B. Potter, ed., *Domestic Law Reforms in Post-Mao China* (Armonk, NY and London: M. E. Sharpe, 1994).
31. For a discussion of the difficulties posed by local protectionism for enforcement of court judgments, see Donald C. Clarke, "Dispute Resolution in China," in 5 *J. Chinese L.* 245 (1991).
32. See 1989 CIETAC Rules, Article 12.
33. See 1989 CIETAC Rules, Article 6.
34. See Pat Chew, "A Procedural and Substantial Analysis of the Fairness of Chinese and Soviet Foreign Trade Arbitration," 21 *Tex. Int'l L. J.* 291 (1986).
35. See CIETAC Rules, Articles 26, et seq.
36. The cooperative relations between CIETAC and the People's Courts, for example, were further undermined by a dispute over the wording of the 1991 Civil Procedure Law over the issue of judicial review of CIETAC arbitral proceedings.
37. See, for example, Matthew Bersani, "Enforcement of Arbitration Awards in China," *China Business Review*, May-June, 1992, p. 6. Also see Bersani, "Enforcement of Arbitration Awards in China," in *International Arbitration*, vol. 10, no. 2 (1993), p. 47.
38. See CPL, Article 259.
39. The convention appears at TIAS 6638, 658 UNTS 163.
40. See TIAS 7444, 847 UNTS 231.
41. See generally, Law Society of China, *Mao Zedong sixiang: Faxue lilun lunwen xuan* (Mao Zedong Thought: Collection of Articles on Legal Thought) (Beijing: 1985). Also see Victor Li, "The Evolution and Development of the Chinese Legal System," in John H. Lindbeck, *CHINA: Management of a Revolutionary Society.*
42. As discussed in the Ministry of Justice's 1980 Report by the Ministry of Justice to the National Conference on Judicial Administrative Work, courts and lawyers were considered to be within the purview of the Ministry's administrative authority. See "Sifabu guanyu quan guo sifa xingzheng gongzuo tanhui de baogao" (Ministry of Justice's 1980 Report to the National Conference of Judicial Administrative Work), in *Zhonghua renmin gongheguo guowuyuan gongbao* (PRC State Council Bulletin) (1980), at pp. 639, 641.
43. See generally, Donald C. Clarke, "Dispute Resolution in China," 5 *J. of Chinese Law* 245 (1991).

Chapter 7

1. See Pitman B. Potter, "The Role of Law in Inducing Foreign Investment into China," 1990 Institute Issue Paper no. 2, Jan. 1992.
2. See chronology of developments in Appendix B.
3. Numerous personal communications during 1987–89 and 1991–93. See Appendix C for a partial list of sources interviewed on a confidential basis during 1991–93. This sentiment has been confirmed most recently by survey results. See "The Council's Investment Initiative," *China Business Review*, Sept.-Oct. 1992, p. 6.

Index

administrative hearings, 83
Administrative Litigation Law (ALL), 9, 41, 62, 83, 85
Administrative Protection of Pharmaceuticals Regulations, 45–46
administrative reform, 8–9
advanced technology enterprises, 40, 46, 58, 59, 65, 66, 85
ALL. *See* Administrative Litigation Law
arbitral awards, 73, 74–75, 77, 79, 86
arbitration, 71–79, 86, 129n10, 129n15, 130n21, 130n24
Association of Southeast Asian Nations (ASEAN), 19

Bank of China, 53, 123nl
Bank of Communications, 55
banking system
  and foreign exchange, 53, 55, 56, 65
  and joint ventures, 27
  legal regime governing the, 27, 124n17
  reform of the, 56, 84, 85
  and representative offices, 27
  and wholly foreign-owned enterprises, 27
  See also People's Bank of China; Bank of China
Beijing, 27, 43
Berne Convention on Protection of Literary and Artistic Works, 45
bilateral treaties, 20, 28, 34, 35, 74, 115n31
black market, 55, 64, 67–68
business taxes, 60–61, 66

Canada, 115n31
CCPIT. *See* China Council for the Promotion of International Trade
cease and desist orders, 85

China Council for the Promotion of International Trade (CCPIT), 71, 78
China International Economic and Trade Arbitration Commission (CIETAC), 71–73, 74, 75, 76–77, 78, 79, 129n15, 131n36
China International Trust and Investment Corporation (CITIC), 55
Civil Procedure Law (CPL), 72, 74, 75, 77, 79, 130n21, 131n36
Coastal Cities, 27, 30, 32, 57–58, 59, 65
commodity inspection system, 10, 11, 14–15, 83
Company Law (1993), 29
computer software, 43, 44, 45
conciliation, 71, 72
Constitution, PRC, 8, 27
consumption taxes, 61
contracts
  and dispute resolution, 75
  dual system of, 35
  and the foreign investment system, 35
  legal regime governing, 7–8
  and policy indeterminacy, 31
  and the trading system, 12, 13, 17–18
  See also Foreign Economic Contract Law (FECL)
cooperative enterprises, 24, 58, 61
cooperative joint ventures, 24, 66, 75
copyrights, 43–45, 47, 84–85
CPL. *See* Civil Procedure Law
credit. *See* loans
customs, 11, 15, 16, 18, 84

Deng Xiaoping, 30–31
development
  and the law, 1–2
  and technology transfers, 49–50
  variation in regional Chinese, 4

About the Publisher

THE 1990 INSTITUTE is a U.S.-based nonprofit research organization dedicated to the study of major economic and social issues relating to China. It was conceived in mid-1989 by a group of volunteers who were deeply concerned about conditions in China and wanted to help the people without getting involved in the politics of either China or the United States.

The Institute's mission is to enhance understanding of the economic and social problems that are impeding China's modernization, and to contribute to the search for their solutions—through independent, objective, and policy-oriented research—for the benefit of the people of China and peace and prosperity of the world. The Institutes sponsors in-depth studies and holds conferences to facilitate an ongoing dialogue between research scholars in the United States and in China.

All research projects of the Institute are guided by four basic principles:

- **Goal orientation** Emphasis on scholarly excellence and practical value;
- **Quality control** All work to be rigorously reviewed by experts;
- **Independence** Political, financial, and intellectual independence from special interests;
- **Objectivity** An open-minded approach and well-balanced presentation.